Through the Customers' Eyes

Improving Your
Company's Results
With the CORe™ Method

Lindsay Geddes

amacom
American Management Association

New York • Atlanta • Boston • Chicago • Kansas City • San Francisco • Washington, D.C.
• Brussels • Toronto • Mexico City

This book is available at a special
discount when ordered in bulk quantities.
For information, contact Special Sales Department,
AMACOM, a division of American Management Association,
135 West 50th Street, New York, NY 10020.

HF
5415.5
G43
1993

Library of Congress Cataloging-in-Publication Data

Geddes, Lindsay.
    Through the customers' eyes : improving your company's results
with the CORe™ method / Lindsay Geddes.
        p.   cm.
    Includes index.
    ISBN 0-8144-5070-9
    1. Customer service. I. Title.
HF5415.G43 1993
658.8'12—dc20   93-6945
                                                             CIP

Printing number

10 9 8 7 6 5 4 3 2 1

To

Reay Geddes,

who showed his children how to think for
ourselves—broadly, constructively, and bravely

and

Douglas Blair Turnbaugh,

for mighty support given with his usual light touch

Contents

Preface

"Pick the future as opposed to the past;
Focus on opportunity rather than on problem;
Choose your own direction—rather than climb on the
    bandwagon; and
Aim high, aim for something that will make a difference,
rather than something that is 'safe' and easy to do."

Peter F. Drucker
The Effective Executive

Accomplishing change that produces bottom-line benefits is probably *the* toughest part of running a business. Regardless of the type of change—operational, strategic, organizational, or a combination—the key is to start with customers.

Orientation to customers isn't for the customers' sake alone, nor because it's fashionable, but because it makes good business sense. Customers are the lifeblood of any business. And the success of any undertaking depends on how well it ties in with customer needs and priorities.

By looking at your company from the outside in, as customers do, you can see it—and its capabilities—in a new light, which can reveal opportunities that perhaps no one in the company was aware of before. This outside-in view also highlights how all parts of the organization must interact for the company to compete effectively, and provides a unifying focal point that people can agree is vital to the company's prosperity.

Knowing the customer viewpoint makes it possible to concentrate efforts and resources where they will have the greatest impact on results. *How to do this* is the principal topic of this book. It describes a concrete step-by-step approach to defining and implementing the changes that will advance your company's standing with customers, strengthen its competitive position, and make the most of its current capabilities and resources. The result? Lasting improvement in financial performance.

This approach, which I developed and named the Customer Orientation for Results (CORe™) Management Method, grew out of my fourteen years' experience in business units of various sizes, and has been honed since. Its purpose is to help solve problems or take advantage of opportunities fully, and it can be used by company and business unit executives alike to make the businesses they run run better.

Through the Customers' Eyes is organized around the method itself. It takes you sequentially through the method, describing and illustrating the contents of each step with examples from various industries. The last section covers how to get started when using the CORe Method.

Two main points make this book especially useful to people concerned with realizing improved results. First, it goes beyond concepts, recommendations, and success stories. These make interesting reading but can leave the results-oriented leader wondering whether and how to apply them in a particular situation. Second, because the CORe Management Method draws from various areas of management and improvement approaches, you will find pulled together here in a streamlined way a number of specific, proven concepts and practices. These include competitive analysis, cross-functional teamwork, niche marketing, financial decision-making, total quality, strategy development, and participative management. The result of this integration is a management tool that I hope you'll find valuable as you lead the way to the accomplishment of changes that produce bottom-line benefits at your company.

It was to make this tool available to people whose working environment and challenges I know firsthand that I wrote this book. I hope it gives you food for thought as well as answers to practical questions—and that your copy quickly becomes dog-eared, indicating that it's being *used*. That, to me, will be the measure of its success.

L.G.

Acknowledgments

The insights and suggestions of many people contributed much to this book and were a great help to me. I appreciate the assistance greatly, especially when it involved voicing less-than-favorable comments and then helping with improvements.

A few people contributed in exceptional, and quite different, ways. For reading the manuscript and making many constructive suggestions, I am particularly grateful to Gene Berger, S. M. Emery, Jim Kent, and Alan Phillips. For help that started before there was a manuscript and continued through its development to completion, special acknowledgment for their contribution goes— along with my heartfelt gratitude—to Melinda Eaton, Bob Ganswindt, Pat Gottfried, Karl Kunz, Andrea Pedolsky, Chris Wagner, and Bob Waugh.

Thank you.

SECTION I
THE FOUNDATION

No matter what the industry, whether in good times or lean, the companies that achieve outstanding financial results aren't necessarily the technology leaders or those with the lowest prices. The key to their success is doing an exceptional job of serving their customers.

Delivering what customers value most in a profitable way may sound straightforward, but it isn't simple or easy. Because different types of customers have different needs and priorities, how a company provides outstanding value varies from one type of customer to the next. And because delivering value to customers is beyond the scope of any one part of a business unit, a concerted effort is needed with all parts of the organization playing the same piece of music.

Attending to internal priorities—those of concern to a particular function, department, or individual—usually takes precedence over serving customers. At most companies, putting customers first in the daily running of a business can be a radical departure from established practice, and approaching problems with customers uppermost in mind is especially unusual. Typical problem-solving measures ignore customers or take them for granted, as Figure I-1 shows. As a result, solutions that are customer-oriented are likely to differ dramatically, in nature and outcome, from courses of action pursued in the past.

Figure I-1. Conventional approaches to common problems.

Situation	Conventional Approaches
Profits fall short of targets	Cut expenses Step up selling efforts Seek new sources of revenue
Market share lost to competitors	Reduce price Step up selling efforts Imitate competitors
Projects produce disappointing results	Intensify pressure Commit more resources Abandon, switch, or add improvement programs
Management team members' views on priorities differ	"Knock heads" or mandate direction Change players Hold team-building sessions

Multiple demands on finite capital raise questions of real need	Use a higher return-on-investment
	  hurdle rate
	Allocate funds based on fairness,
	  gut feelings, or internal politics
	  or preferences

Setting out to beat certain competitors—which may or may not be considered front-runners by customers—on matters of little importance to customers is a losing proposition. Concentrating on competitors rather than customers is the equivalent of trying to run the opposing team off the field rather than move the ball closer to the goal. For example, in the 1970s and 1980s, banks and credit card companies that battled one another to lend money—in real estate, to developing countries, and to consumers—ended up with port-folios loaded with nonperforming loans that seriously damaged their financial performance.

Other courses of action that produce mixed results at best involve solutions that worked for the company in the past or that worked for other companies. Using measures that worked in different circumstances is a hit-or-miss proposition, as more and more companies are discovering. For example:

▲ A particular improvement approach—such as just-in-time, concurrent engineering, or computer integrated manufacturing—may or may not tie in with customers' priorities, meaning that resources are focused where they might have little impact. And solving a problem in one area can cause another to crop up elsewhere, making bottom-line benefits elusive.

▲ Broad-brush improvement approaches—so-called big fixes such as organizational change programs, total quality management, and business reengineering—are inherently resource-consuming and slow. Their sheer magnitude implies months of preparation and education, extensive administration, and years before bottom-line benefits show—if the momentum of so massive an undertaking can be maintained. Companywide efforts can be the equivalent of dismantling and reassembling an automobile when all that's needed is an engine overhaul.

If the solution to a business problem is to have the earliest possible positive and lasting impact on financial results, it must—by definition—be customized to customers and the company itself. The overriding consideration when setting out to solve a problem, or to enhance financial performance, must therefore be this: how best to serve high-potential customers—whether current or new—by building on the company's present capabilities and so make the best use of all its resources.

Constructing original solutions to build on a company's strengths and help an organization work as a cohesive whole to serve customers more effectively and profitably is what this book is about. It is for people who are responsible—and who feel responsible—for results and seek to improve them. Completing the questionnaire in Figure I-2 will give you an indication of how customer-oriented your organization is.

The approach described in this book—the Customer Orientation for Results (CORe) Method—is not a program to be imple-

Figure I-2. Self-assessment questionnaire: how customer-oriented are we?

Indicators	Don't Know	Never	Rarely	Some-times	Often	Always
1. We seek input from customers who buy from us and who buy from competitors to be sure we understand how customers choose their suppliers, how they think we need to improve, and how their needs are changing.	___	___	___	___	___	___
2. Our managers in all functions consider what matters most to customers when setting priorities, giving direction and support, and solving problems.	___	___	___	___	___	___
3. What customers say about how we stack up against our competitors focuses our search for ways to operate more effectively in all departments.	___	___	___	___	___	___
4. We direct our product development efforts to reflect customers' views on new products, prototypes, and proposed revisions.	___	___	___	___	___	___
5. Our business plans, marketing plans, and proposals for capital spending target high-potential customer groups selected for fit with our capabilities.	___	___	___	___	___	___
6. People throughout our organization work together with customers in mind whether performing day-to-day activities or working on projects, and are rewarded accordingly.	___	___	___	___	___	___
7. Our performance measurements in all departments include customers' criteria for choosing and retaining suppliers.	___	___	___	___	___	___
8. We track the bottom-line contribution of sales to different customer groups.	___	___	___	___	___	___

mented. Rather, the CORe Method is a management tool that uses orientation to customers to address business issues in ways that produce lasting and positive impacts on profits and investment returns.

Introduction to the CORe Method

The CORe Method was designed by and for people in line positions to help them decide on direction and accomplish results-oriented action throughout the business unit. Organizationwide orientation to customers and profits is the underlying theme of the CORe Method, and lasting improvement in financial performance is the ultimate objective. The steps that make up the CORe Method are fitted together to achieve that end, as shown in the diagram in Figure I-3. Collectively, these steps make it possible to focus a business on the key market areas and the key internal changes. This maximizes the potential improvement in financial results.

The CORe Method has four steps:

Step One The Context: Understanding Customer Viewpoints
Step Two Concreteness: Scoping Out Needed Changes
Step Three The Crux: Establishing the New Direction
Step Four The Culmination: Working Together for Customers and Profits

Each step is essential for different reasons. The heart of the method is Step Three. Steps One and Two lead up to it, providing information that is essential to sound decision making at the business unit (or company) management level. Step Four produces results. Figure I-4 shows how these four steps connect.

Step One: The Context. Step One reveals the types of customers that offer a company the best profit potential and what *they* perceive as the company's strengths and weaknesses.

In Step One, you learn directly from customers which product and service attributes add up to exceptional value and how well they think their suppliers—including your company—are performing. The customer viewpoint is then used to assess key

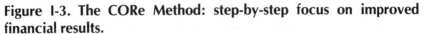

Figure I-3. The CORe Method: step-by-step focus on improved financial results.

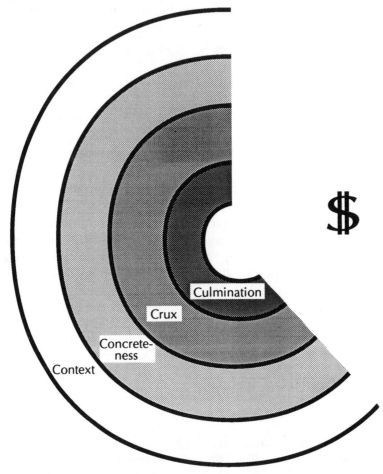

competitors' capabilities and actions. Thus, the focus of Step One is outside the company with an eye to the future.

Step Two: Concreteness. Step Two brings the customer perspective inside the organization to determine what it would take to accomplish the changes needed for the company to excel in their eyes.

In Step Two, you define the key changes needed based on what you learned from customers in Step One. You determine how

Figure I-4. Overview of the CORe Method.

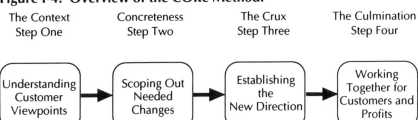

The Context	Concreteness	The Crux	The Culmination
Step One	Step Two	Step Three	Step Four

Understanding Customer Viewpoints → Scoping Out Needed Changes → Establishing the New Direction → Working Together for Customers and Profits

Copyright © 1992 Lindsay Geddes

best to accomplish these changes and define the actions and gauge the time and resources required. Involving people from all organizational levels spreads awareness of customers and of the need for change and produces proposals that are known to be applicable and workable. This involvement counteracts NIH (not-invented-here) resistance and inertia with a sense of ownership and urgency.

The information on internal changes from Step Two and information on the overall market, customers, and competitors from Step One together provide the basis for decision making.

Step Three: The Crux. Step Three produces decisions on direction and target performance levels—in terms of customers and financial results—and sets the stage for successful implementation.

In Step Three, you determine how best to position the company in the eyes of customers in a market area that offers it attractive profit potential. This target market position indicates what the business unit needs to work on first to become or remain a leading supplier and realize higher profits and investment returns. Shaping an implementation plan for all functions leads to revision of resource allocations and financial targets. You then make the organizational adjustments needed to foster collaborative, customer-oriented action. Active participation of all members of the management team ensures that the best possible decisions on direction are taken and engenders broad commitment to achieve targeted results. With the overall direction set, the focus shifts to implementation.

Step Four: The Culmination. Step Four converts plans into action, progress, and improved results.

Building on the customer awareness and sense of urgency and ownership initiated in Step Two, you now spread understanding of what the company aims to achieve and how, and you form the teams responsible for implementing the action plan. You support and guide the teams, ensuring that their efforts, day-to-day activities, and any other projects proceed in concert to achieve target levels of performance.

During implementation and afterwards, reviewing market developments and revisiting earlier steps capitalize on the company's enhanced market standing and increased ability to accomplish productive change. Use of the CORe Method is, therefore, iterative.

The thread running through all four steps to connect customers and profits is the concept of customer value. Finding out in Step One what constitutes outstanding value for customers provides a framework for the work done in the other steps, resulting in the delivery of superior value. How the customer value concept applies in each step is shown in Figure I-5.

The CORe Method encompasses several areas of management. The power of the CORe Method is not in the novelty of its parts but in the way it integrates tried-and-true concepts and practices that are usually treated separately, such as competitive analysis, financial decision making, and participative management. The concept of a whole being greater than the sum of its

Figure I-5. Customer value—the connecting thread.

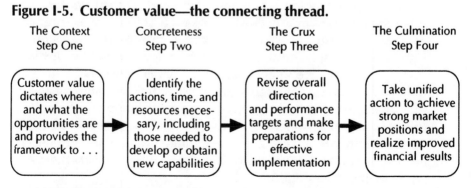

The Context Step One	Concreteness Step Two	The Crux Step Three	The Culmination Step Four
Customer value dictates where and what the opportunities are and provides the framework to . . .	Identify the actions, time, and resources necessary, including those needed to develop or obtain new capabilities	Revise overall direction and performance targets and make preparations for effective implementation	Take unified action to achieve strong market positions and realize improved financial results

parts is well established. However, it implies that the parts are modified to fit together in a streamlined way. Familiar topics may therefore appear to be different and occur in a different sequence from usual.

Issues the CORe Method Helps Resolve

Using the CORe Method helps resolve a variety of issues, such as the following:

▲ Anticipating customers' changing priorities and needs to become or remain a preferred supplier

▲ Overcoming competitive pressures and achieving positive nonprice differentiation

▲ Tightening the focus on current products or markets to make the most productive use of existing resources

▲ Channeling all departments' time and energy into working together to serve customers

▲ Getting floundering or disappointing improvement efforts back on track

▲ Capitalizing on market opportunities to take advantage of company strengths and improve profitability with limited new investment

▲ Deciding how best to invest financial resources: in R&D? Manufacturing? Acquisitions? Computerized information systems?

▲ Developing and launching new and revised products and services effectively and efficiently

▲ Designing the fastest and most cost-effective program to realize lasting operational improvements, such as speeding delivery, upgrading quality, and reducing cost

▲ Pursuing growth initiatives for the future while maintaining a high level of service to current customers

▲ Stemming and reversing a loss of business in a particular market

▲ Deciding whether to enter an attractive market area or remain in one that's declining

You may, of course, be facing issues not on this list, such as responding to changes in customers' purchasing practices or considering whether to embark on a joint venture or build an overseas presence.

Precise definition and classification of an issue aren't necessary to determine whether the CORe Method will be helpful. If resolving the issue affects or involves customers or profits, it will be.

Narrower classification risks a grave misperception: that what's really a matter for a whole business unit can be addressed by a particular function or department—such as human resources (organizational issues) or product management (marketing issues). This increases the likelihood that parts of the organization will trip over one another in pursuit of disparate priorities. Delegation of responsibility for what is really a general management issue amounts to passing the buck and decreases the chances of actually solving the problem.

Don't be alarmed because some of the issues listed above appear "strategic." This doesn't mean that you'll have to struggle with elaborate quantitative decision-making models, esoteric language, and lengthy paperwork. Nor does it imply embarking on pie-in-the-sky propositions (entering a glamorous, high-growth market area full of strong competitors where, as a latecomer, your company would be among the also-rans) or pursuing courses of action that cannot succeed (adding product features and options when customers need a stripped-down, easy-to-use version). Avoiding such time- and resource-draining exercises is one of the advantages of using the CORe Method. With it, you find out ahead of time what you're getting into; only if there's truly an opportunity for your company do you proceed to capitalize on it.

The pragmatism inherent in the CORe Method means that you don't need an advanced academic degree and the brainpower of a rocket scientist to understand and use it effectively. However, getting the most from the CORe Method calls for three things, which are not for the fainthearted:

1. Listening—to customers and to people inside the organization, even at the lowest levels, when what you hear may be tough to swallow

2. Making far-reaching decisions—about the types of customers, the actions to be taken, and who's really best qualified to play a certain part, when these decisions imply departing from what's comfortable or spurning what you advocated in the past
3. Providing hands-on leadership of results-oriented action (that is, initiating, tracking, supporting, spurring on, and rewarding progress) when handing off responsibility to someone who reports to you or to a staff department is a tempting way to limit your personal risk

These things—and, by implication, the willingness to think—are prerequisites for making the most of the CORe Method, which is why this book is for people who are and *feel* responsible for results.

What's Next

The next section describes the CORe Method, drawing on situations from real companies for illustration. The examples serve only to illustrate points, not to recommend specific courses of action or to presuppose particular outcomes. The appropriate solution and attainable outcomes at your company depend on its situation at the time and are for you to determine.

Because the CORe Method is distinctive in encompassing a range of concepts and practices, this book emphasizes their integration—the forest rather than the individual trees. This focus on the big picture avoids dwelling on areas that have been written about extensively elsewhere. Some parts of the CORe Method, however, are described in greater detail than others. These parts cover topics that are rarely written about, or rarely written about in a sufficiently pragmatic way, or are especially problematic in practice.

The last section of the book describes getting started with the CORe Method. How you use it depends on the decisions or issues being faced and how far along you are with them. This section includes a summary format to help you keep track of the work in each step and estimations of the time it typically involves.

▲   ▲   ▲

Now to the description of the CORe Method. If you have a specific business issue in mind it will be easier to see how and when using the CORe Method would be helpful. The issue might be a new one or one on which work is already under way and for which some solutions may have been tried without success. Bearing this issue in mind as you read can raise questions or considerations that might have been overlooked, giving you insight into tackling and resolving the issue in reality. You can use the recap after each step to note the immediate tasks needed to resolve your issue.

SECTION II
THE
METHODOLOGY

Step One

The Context: Understanding Customer Viewpoints

In Step One, you identify where and what the external opportunities and challenges are for your company. You start by taking an objective look at the market from the end-user perspective to determine the impact of market developments on your business. This leads to identification of the market areas that offer the best profit potential for your company—the areas where your high-potential customers are. You then develop an in-depth understanding of the customer perspective in one or more of these market areas. This information is then used to evaluate competitors.

Making customers the focal point of market analysis provides the information you need to decide on direction and to focus efforts and resources on activities that will lead to higher profits and investment returns. Focusing market analysis on customers also streamlines it. Early identification of the types of customers you'll do research on produces insight into their perspective sooner and more efficiently. And being fully informed about the customers' perspective allows you to focus analysis of competitors on the key ones and their main strengths and weaknesses.

▲   ▲   ▲

Step One has four parts:

Part A Bird's-Eye View of the Market
Part B The High-Potential Customer

15

/ *Part C* Customers' Viewpoint
\ *Part D* Customer Orientation of Competitors

The contents of this step and how it connects with others are shown in Figure 1-1.

The information developed in Step One makes it possible to answer questions about the market in general, about certain customers, and about the competition. Examples of such questions are:

The Market

▲ Where will product demand be greatest in the future—two to five years from now?
▲ What is the market potential for our products or services?
▲ Are current distributors reaching end users where demand is growing?
▲ Are there potential customers that we aren't currently marketing to?
▲ What market growth can we now expect in our core business?

Customers

▲ What should we be doing differently to serve customers more effectively?
▲ Are customers' needs changing? If so, in what way?
▲ Do our key customers have needs that neither we nor our competitors are meeting?
▲ Which types of customers would be most receptive to the products we have in R&D?
▲ What do our biggest customers think that our strengths and weaknesses are? What do they think are the competition's?
▲ What opportunities—other than price reductions—are there to differentiate our company from competitors?
▲ How do customers make their purchase decisions? What criteria matter most?
▲ How do customers view our performance compared with that of other suppliers?

Figure 1-1. Step One—The Context: Understanding Customer Viewpoints.

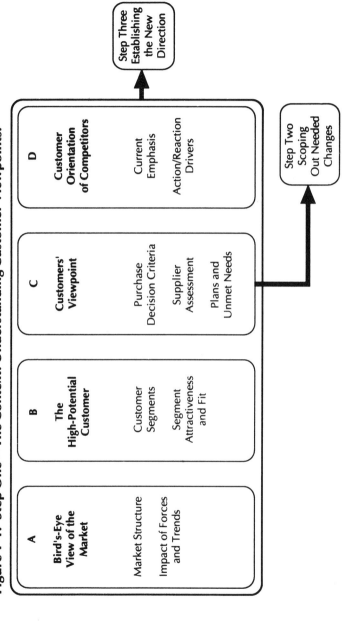

A	B	C	D
Bird's-Eye View of the Market	The High-Potential Customer	Customers' Viewpoint	Customer Orientation of Competitors
Market Structure	Customer Segments	Purchase Decision Criteria	Current Emphasis
Impact of Forces and Trends	Segment Attractiveness and Fit	Supplier Assessment	Action/Reaction Drivers
		Plans and Unmet Needs	

Step Two Scoping Out Needed Changes

Step Three Establishing the New Direction

Competitors

▲ Who is our competition?
▲ How is a competitor's restructuring, addition to sales force, etc. likely to help or hinder its standing with customers?
▲ Other than new products that we hear about through the grapevine, what are our competitors working on that we should be aware of?
▲ How can certain competitors get products to market so fast? Offer lower prices? Deliver so promptly?
▲ Which competitors are likely to present the greatest threat in the future?

The Key to Bottom-Line Benefits: Customer Knowledge

You probably have at least one improvement effort—a product launch, a marketing campaign to attract new customers, a manufacturing investment—under way or under consideration. What appears to be a straightforward, go/no-go decision is made complex by its ramifications. Will the project offer an adequate return on the resources committed to it? What are its merits compared with those of other projects? Finally, what about the trade-off between the project and the day-to-day activities that keep orders from current customers coming in, current products moving out, near-term revenue flowing in, and profits accumulating? Overlooking this trade-off when deciding on resource allocations is likely to cause confusion over priorities. It is also likely to overload some resources and underutilize others. A fundamental, unifying concept simplifies decision making significantly: *For day-to-day activities and improvement projects alike, the principal focus must be on customers.* This concept sounds obvious, but most companies only pay lip service to it.

Consider how few projects produce the hoped-for impact on profits. However and wherever resources are invested—in warehouse equipment, sales coverage, computers, operational improvements, product development, training programs, joint ventures, sales promotions, or international expansion—it is *customers* who actually generate profits, cash flow, and returns. Which customers and which product and service attributes to invest in must, therefore, be the primary consideration when deciding on direction and priorities. But the customer information needed to make these decisions isn't in a book you can take off the shelf. It has to be developed.

Results-oriented people usually consider analysis to be a necessary evil at best. Yet the soundness of a decision and people's confidence in it ride on the quality of the information on which it is based. Experienced judgment is priceless, but it is no substitute for comprehensive, up-to-date facts. Information deficiencies that force reliance on opinion, gut feelings, and hurried back-of-the-envelope calculations undermine the success of an undertaking before it even gets started. Bad decisions such as the following can result:

▲ Committing resources to a market area whose growth rate isn't high enough to generate the cash flow needed to realize desired returns, no matter what market share you achieve

▲ Emphasizing pricing when customers' primary concern after product performance is prompt delivery, and competitors are improving their turnaround time by leaps and bounds

▲ Embarking on a program to cut manufacturing lead time when the key to advancing your standing with customers is prompt and reliable communication with them

▲ Taking resources away from activities that provide customers with the products and services they value

It is obvious that these undertakings don't make sense. But even a decision maker who is perfectly logical and spends a considerable amount of time with customers may be off the mark for a number of reasons. For example:

▲ Customers often keep suppliers off guard by carping about price when other issues are of equal or greater importance.

▲ So much emphasis may be placed on *current* customers that market areas with perhaps greater profit potential remain unexplored.

▲ A competitor's action, a vendor problem, or internal matters can easily detract attention from customers.
▲ People inside the organization may be reluctant to speak up when a course of action being discussed doesn't make sense.

As a result, companies can unwittingly pursue endeavors that lack significance to customers and bottom-line results.

More important than avoiding what doesn't make sense is defining the initiatives that *do* tie in with high-potential customers' priorities and company realities and that *will* produce the desired financial results and move the company closer to its goals.

Decisions made using the CORe Method are based on a fresh look at the business in terms of customers: their prospects, needs, priorities, and assessment of the company's strengths and weaknesses. Thus, the information developed in Step One is much more in-depth than customary market research such as that done to test product concepts, refine sales promotion programs, or calculate investment paybacks. In industrial businesses especially, market research often goes no further than direct customers, bypassing consideration of these customers' customers and, possibly, their customers—the end users. The thrust of customary market research is usually to obtain information related to predetermined actions and expenditures. With the CORe Method, however, you start with a clean slate, setting out to understand the customer perspective and then to determine the actions and expenditures that will be beneficial and make decisions accordingly.

The market analysis done with the CORe Method provides fresh, meaty information that reveals what's behind statistics such as market size and growth rate and customers' decisions among suppliers. In addition to its use for decision making, this information about customers lets you demonstrate to them your interest in their business, and respond promptly to changes in their needs.

Part A: Bird's-Eye View of the Market

First you develop an overview of the market structure and determine the effects that key forces and trends are likely to have on your business. This overview encompasses market areas the company currently serves as well as those it does not. Part A is highlighted in Figure 1-2.

▲   ▲   ▲

The further removed a company is from end users, the easier it is to lose track of who uses its products and how. Yet end-user needs and preferences have a ripple effect back through the supply chain, influencing the sources and nature of demand on manufacturers and their suppliers. Thus, by reviewing what end users' and the intermediaries' needs and preferences are likely to be, you gain insight into what lies ahead for your company.

Mapping the Supply Chain
From End Users to Your Company

Viewing the market as if from a helicopter lets you take an objective look at the lay of the land. Identifying the various links in the supply chain and the connections among them shows where your company fits in the chain. The number of links varies from industry to industry but can include suppliers of raw materials, manufacturers, assemblers, distributors, wholesalers, retail outlets, and end users. You may do business at several levels. For example, a supplier of parts used in capital goods might serve some manufacturers directly as well as some distributors that supply other manufacturers and end users.

Ultimately, demand for almost all products is determined by consumer households, but end users of your products might be government bodies, corporations, nonprofit organizations, and professional firms. Working back along the chain from each type of end user to determine what that purchaser at each level seeks and from where (instead of what your company sells and to whom) verifies that you've identified all the relevant channels and links between end users and your company.

This big-picture look at the supply chain from the end users' point of view can reveal new applications for your products or additional ways to serve current customers. For example, a company making adhesives for use with rubber realized that home-

Figure 1-2. Step One—The Context: Understanding Customer Viewpoints, Part A.

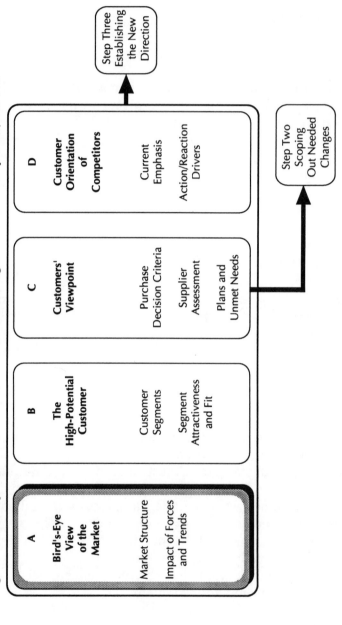

repair kits for bicycle tires were a source of demand it had not explored. And a subcontract manufacturer for the defense industry saw another way to serve its customers by assisting them with the development of manufacturing processes for new products. Charting the supply chain from end users to your company (see Figure 1-3) lets you see at a glance the overall market structure and the various sources of demand for your products.

With the current market structure laid out, you determine the relative significance of different channels and end users by piecing together information you already have, augmented by publicly available data. Sources include trade association publications and magazine articles, market research firm surveys, and government reports, such as those from the Department of Commerce. Estimates extracted from such sources indicate the total demand for certain products and the percentage flowing through certain channels.

This information can put internal breakdowns of sales revenue into proper perspective, possibly for the first time. Market share data are easy to come by in certain businesses, especially at the consumer mass-market level, but are often patchy or nonexistent further back in the supply chain.

Figure 1-3. Sample layout for supply chain.

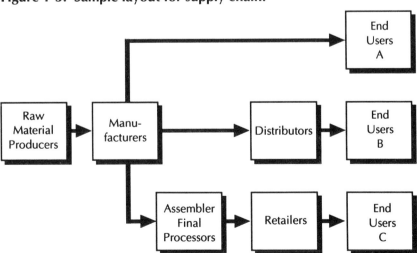

Adding figures about overall demand and its breakdown to the market overview chart gives you a baseline to help determine the significance of likely changes.

Viewing the Future Market

Identifying the forces and trends that affect your industry and assessing their likely impact come next. The relevance of specific forces and trends varies from industry to industry, but there are only three general types:

1. *Demographics and life-style changes,* such as the percentage of the population in certain age groups and increased interest in health and fitness
2. *Sociopolitical changes and regulatory and environmental considerations,* such as shifts to free-market economies, to tighter requirements that a finished product contain parts manufactured in the country where it's sold, and away from use of certain manufacturing ingredients
3. *Broad trends,* such as globalization, economic conditions, and technological developments, which are evidenced by, for example, increased worldwide travel and growth in the use of electronic communications

Having identified the key trends that apply, you trace back along the supply chain from end users to determine the effects on your company. You can predict purchasers' likely responses by considering the actions you'd take if you were in their place. Remaining objective when considering the impacts can be tough. The tendency is to see change as negative. But keeping an open mind lets you see how certain changes may actually be to your advantage.

Deregulation, reductions in government spending, and a weak economy bring cost pressures that affect purchasers and suppliers at various levels, which sounds like bad news. Yet the ripple effects can be positive. For example:

▲ When consumers delay replacement of expensive durable goods, the demand for replacement parts and repair services increases.

▲ Manufacturers using subcontractors are likely to bring work back in-house to spread the costs of their current capacity. However, they may seek to make certain overhead costs variable by farming out activities not central to their business.

▲ Companies supplying overseas markets might opt for local sourcing to avoid transportation costs. However, this offers their current suppliers a low-risk way of entering a new market by setting up an offshore facility to serve them.

▲ When smaller companies participate in group purchasing for volume discounts, the formerly prohibitive cost of serving them individually no longer applies. This opens up another potential source of profits.

Should the impact of market changes imply challenges, knowing about them in advance allows you to avoid being caught off guard and having to react defensively. With time to think ahead, plan, and act accordingly, you can convert a potential setback into an opportunity. For example, machine tool builders that failed to recognize the trend toward computerized manufacturing found themselves in a catch-up position, especially vulnerable to strong competition from overseas. But the companies that saw how computerization would affect their business used this insight to plan; they set out to convert their products, determined whether to supply separate pieces of equipment or turnkey systems, and selected the overseas markets to pursue.

Since interpretation of trends is crucial, you may want to confirm or augment your conclusions by checking them against published growth rates and market size projections from different sources and by reviewing your reasoning with a couple of industry experts. You can then revise and annotate the market overview chart.

▲　　▲　　▲

Having taken an objective look at the market structure and assessed the impact of key forces and trends, you now carve from this big picture groups of customers that can be served in similar ways.

Part B: The High-Potential Customer

To determine the types of customers that offer the best profit potential for your business, you segment the overall market into distinct customer groups and short-list them in light of their inherent attractiveness and according to their fit with your company's capabilities. From this shortlist, you select the customer segments to be explored in depth. Part B is highlighted in Figure 1-4.

▲   ▲   ▲

Realistically, no company can serve all customers equally effectively and profitably. Some customers are better positioned for the future, and some have needs that your company is more or less able to fill right now. The tighter the focus on attractive customer segments where the company's current capabilities fit well, the more productively its resources will be deployed and the greater the impact on profits. Proper definition of customer segments is therefore your starting point toward realizing lasting profit improvement. Proper segmentation also provides a framework for defining the direction that will make the most of current strengths and resources.

Questioning Current Market Breakdowns

Breaking down the market in terms of customers' characteristics, needs, and buying practices strikes a happy medium between serving each customer in a unique way and serving all customers in the same way. This also allows you to determine the types of customers that offer the best profit potential. Just as a dollar in revenue from different products yields different gross margins, a dollar in sales from certain types of customers yields different bottom-line results. Being selective helps avoid proliferation of marginally profitable customers and products. Because companies that define their markets in customers' terms are the rare exception, this grouping is likely to differ from market breakdowns you currently use.

Defining a company's market in terms of industries served or products sold says little about customers. A definition such as "we

Figure 1-4. Step One—The Context: Understanding Customer Viewpoints, Part B.

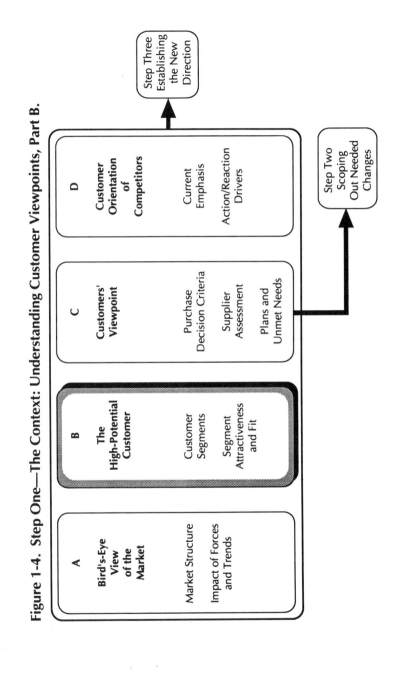

A

Bird's-Eye View of the Market

Market Structure

Impact of Forces and Trends

B

The High-Potential Customer

Customer Segments

Segment Attractiveness and Fit

C

Customers' Viewpoint

Purchase Decision Criteria

Supplier Assessment

Plans and Unmet Needs

D

Customer Orientation of Competitors

Current Emphasis

Action/Reaction Drivers

Step Three
Establishing the New Direction

Step Two
Scoping Out Needed Changes

serve the appliance, automotive, and health care industries" leaves unanswered major questions about customers: Do they provide products or services? Make original equipment or serve the after-market? Act as intermediaries or serve end users directly?

A market breakdown in terms of product volumes has similar drawbacks. *Market* has come to mean the measurable demand for certain products, and *segment* to mean the demand for a subset of products. At one time, the worldwide *market* for computer printers was $30 billion and that for computerized data-storage devices approximately $50 billion; a certain disk-drive *segment* accounted for 10 percent of the latter. Such quantitative, product-based market definitions gloss over the crucial consideration of who buys the product, masking the fact that customers' purchases cut across product categories. And such definitions give no indication of why and where purchases are made.

Classifying customers in terms of their significance to the company, according to the sales revenue they currently represent, almost certainly encompasses different types of purchasers. The top 20 percent of a supplier's customers—its key accounts—might include manufacturers, distributors, and even business units within the same customer company. A market breakdown in terms of customer size or location says little about their needs. More important is knowing that, for example, certain purchasers are looking for standard or custom products, versatility through fea-tures and options, or stripped-down products for simplicity of use and maintenance. Thus, segmenting the market in customers' terms produces groupings that are relevant to your company that you can use in determining how best to market to and serve them.

Seeing Your Market in Terms of Customers— and Customer Value

Proper segmentation is a matter of logic and business judg-ment supported by facts and analysis. The key is using information about purchasers to see how distinctions and similarities among them determine their buying patterns and priorities. *A supplier typically thinks in terms of the products or services it provides. Customers think in terms of the value they receive.*

The more functional a product, the more purchasers seek value that can be defined and measured. Products marketed business to business are sold almost exclusively on economic value. But from the customer perspective, the product itself is only one aspect of value and, therefore, of limited significance in purchase decisions. This is true for finished products (both durable and nondurable goods) and for intermediate products (parts, components, subassemblies, and materials that purchasers use in the manufacture, assembly, or maintenance of finished products).

Study after study has shown that factors other than product and price are key considerations in what constitutes value to customers, carrying as much as 70 percent weight in purchase decisions. Failing to recognize the significance of nonproduct and nonprice considerations, a manufacturer of aircraft engines lost one of its most important customers—a foreign airline based in a part of the world where air travel was growing by leaps and bounds. Receiving one late shipment after another, the foreign airline switched its business to another manufacturer.

To customers—whether end users, distributors, or manufacturers—value is a package. With the CORe Method, this value package has four elements: the Product, the Transaction, Support, and Pricing* (Figure 1-5). These customer value elements are expanded on and used in Part C and are used in the other three steps as well.

Defining Relevant Distinctions Among Customers

Customers with different characteristics have different needs and buying patterns, meaning that the significance they attach to each value element differs. For each type of product, therefore, the first cut at classifying customers is according to what they do with it: purchase for end use, for incorporation into products they make (assembly or further processing), or for resale in its current form.

When customers are assemblers or resellers, you can make distinctions among them by considering how their customers use

---

*Throughout this book, these words are capitalized when they are used to refer to the customer value elements defined in the CORe Method.

Figure 1-5. Customer value: a four-part package.

Customer Value Element	Examples of Element Composition
Product	Product and package performance characteristics Options and customization
Transaction	Presale inquiries and order placement/ contract procedures Product delivery Billing accuracy
Support	Sales and marketing assistance and materials Product use and maintenance assistance, including documentation and spares Product development assistance Assistance with improvement programs, regulatory and environmental matters
Pricing	Net purchase price Replacement, warranty, return policies Payment/financing options and terms

the finished product. Assemblers might specialize in serving customers who need products for indoor use as well as other customers needing products that stand up to extended use in tough weather conditions. Each application calls for certain product performance criteria (e.g., reliability, durability) and features (e.g., lightweight or watertight casings), which affect what assemblers and resellers are looking for.

Even when the product itself is the same, end-user characteristics can affect what assemblers and resellers seek. These characteristics include the nature of end-user operations and their familiarity with the product. Resellers might serve commercial firms that use products to provide repair services as well as end users who do their own maintenance. Resellers' large-scale end-use customers and repair-business customers probably buy large quantities of a number of frequently used parts, care little about the appearance of packaging, and expect low per-unit prices. In this instance, the Transaction and Pricing are more important than the Product; Support is relatively unimportant. But to a reseller's small-scale end-use customers, limited quantities of certain products, instructions and advice in their use, and attractive-looking packaging are likely to be important; per-unit price is a lesser consideration. In this situation, Support is as important as the Product, with Pricing and the Transaction carrying less weight.

End-use product characteristics and the characteristics of end users themselves help distinguish among customers within the three basic categories of purchasers (end users, assemblers or further processors, and resellers) and the weight they attach to the four value elements. There may be characteristics of intermediaries and end users that represent finer distinctions, such as language differences, financial condition, and age group or educational level of users. But such distinctions may be inherent in those already defined. The point is not to subdivide the market as finely as possible but to define groups according to distinctions that are significant to customers and the company.

This can mean that parts of the same company belong in different customer groups. For example, a manufacturer of food preparation equipment found that parts of a major hotel, restaurant, and food service company have less in common with one another than with their counterparts at other companies. More specifically, the customer company's airport catering has less in common with the hotel restaurants owned by the company than with chains of restaurants and fast-food outlets owned by other companies.

Grouping Customers by Similarities

With distinctions among purchasers defined, you may see ways to pull together groups according to similarities. Although the groupings must recognize differences in customer needs and buying practices, assembling groups on the basis of some commonality can legitimately reduce the number of customer segments. For example, end users who buy directly might fall into three categories, such as corporate offices, schools, and hospitals. But buying practices at for-profit schools and hospitals may have less in common with their not-for-profit counterparts than with corporate offices. In this instance, direct purchasers might be better defined as two customer segments: for-profit and not-for-profit.

As long as the product and its application are the same, grouping end users served by the same distribution channel might also be valid. This means that purchasers in different countries, but in a geographic or trading bloc served by a certain channel, might belong in the same customer segment.

There is no one right way to group customers. Breaking your market into customer segments is largely a matter of using information about purchasers logically and applying business common sense. Thus, the definition of customer segments is likely to be based on a combination of classifications. These might be the types of product sought; end-use application; whether purchasers are end users, manufacturers or assemblers, distributors, or service providers; whether purchaser organizations are large or small; and where purchasers are located—whether in a certain geographic region or at a certain distance from company facilities. The characteristics and buying patterns of the customer segments you've defined and the relative importance of the value elements to each segment can be captured on a chart such as that in Figure 1-6.

Reviewing the chart can validate the groupings. When customers are properly grouped, the relative significance of the value elements seems self-evident in light of the customer characteristics and buying practices in each segment. It's logical, for example, that purchasers that order small quantities of custom products tend to put greater emphasis on technical support and attach less importance to early delivery and price. And purchasers that themselves have a large customer base and use high volumes of standard products are likely to attach the greatest importance to on-time delivery and low price, putting less emphasis on technical support.

Just as there is no one right way to segment your market, there is no right number of segments. However, one customer segment is too few. It suggests that the segment has been defined too broadly. Moreover, serving only one customer segment carries significant business risk. Three or more segments allow room for selection.

Figure 1-6. Customer segment distinctions—lubricant manufacturer.

Customer Segment	Distinctive Buying Factors	Customer Value Element Importance			
		Product	Transac-tion	Support	Pricing
Manufacturers/assemblers of, automobiles off-road equipment	Deliver to forecast, with some flexibility Large quantities of standard products (for current models only) Consistent product quality New model development support only Increasingly price/internal cost-conscious	M	H	M–L	M–H
Large servicers of original equipment: fleet owners, car dealerships	Formulation/container size for current and older models, for specific makes Variable quantities hard to predict, hold limited inventory, immediate delivery of emergency orders Some technical problem solving	M	M–H	L	L
Aftermarket distributors	High, predictable volumes Ordering/shipping efficiency Quantities packaged for breakdown/retail sale Highly price-sensitive	L	H	L	M–H
Manufacturers/assemblers of custom engineered products for mining, civil engineering	Heavy product design support Job-dependent quantities Longer lead times acceptable but on-time delivery Pricing per job	H	L	H	L

Key: H = High, M = Medium, L = Low

Screening Customer Segments for Profit Potential

A customer segment's profit potential for a particular company is based on the segment's inherent attractiveness and how well the company's current capabilities fit there. Assessing profit potential at this stage is primarily to screen out any segments in which potential is poor. A customer segment with medium or high profit potential for your company is a candidate for further exploration before deciding whether and how best to commit resources to it.

Considering a customer segment's inherent attractiveness is a safeguard against a dangerous assumption: that a segment in which the company's current capabilities apply is automatically one in which it's desirable to do business. This assumption carries the risk of investing where the potential for financial returns is unacceptably low.

Objective assessment of segment attractiveness includes review of the market statistics and qualitative information developed in Part A. The first consideration in this assessment is segment size and growth. A segment made up of purchasers favorably affected by market trends (e.g., manufacturers of computer network devices, distributors of do-it-yourself home-improvement supplies, administrators of retirement homes) is likely to have an attractive near-term growth rate.

The second indicator of relative attractiveness is typical profit margin in the segment. Estimates of how a dollar spent by the end user breaks down into margins and costs at different links in the supply chain reveal where margins are greatest. Multiple links imply slim margins. Because gross margin estimates can be misleading, operating margins—after sales and service expenses—are a better indicator of a segment's attractiveness, especially when pre- and postsale support is highly significant, product development costs are high, or large shipments paid for by the supplier go to remote locations.

The last key consideration in segment attractiveness is the degree of competition, both current and future. The existence of many entrenched suppliers usually makes a segment less attractive. And a segment in which purchasers are consolidating means fewer customers with greater purchasing power and increased competition among existing suppliers.

A segment is therefore inherently attractive when it is sizable and has a moderate or better growth rate, or when it is smaller but growing fast, and has moderate or better profit margins and few competitors or established competitors that are complacent.

But even a highly attractive segment is not necessarily a good opportunity for the company. The fit between the capabilities needed to serve a customer segment and the company's current ability to do so must be considered. The better the fit, the greater the potential for realizing higher profits relatively soon and with limited new investment. The capabilities associated with serving different segments can vary significantly but can usually be deduced by reviewing the characteristics and buying patterns of each segment and the relative significance of the value elements. For example, the need for product customization calls for product design expertise; the manufacture of certain types of products requires specific technological capabilities; and prompt supply calls for adequate production capacity.

Equally significant are less concrete considerations involving the company's own roots and traits. These need particular scrutiny when assessing a customer segment other than the company's current core business. Objectivity is crucial. Even when the basic capabilities called for in a new segment (product development and manufacturing capabilities, sales, distribution, and service coverage) are present, lack of specific knowledge or experience can be a hurdle. For example:

▲ To a company accustomed to negotiated pricing for custom products, the pricing and costing of standard products is a different matter. This situation applies, for example, to a company based in the defense industry branching out into commercial businesses.

▲ For a company whose roots are in the advertising and promotion of a few high-technology and proprietary products, these roots could be a drawback to serving customers that seek a range of undifferentiated products at competitive prices. This situation applies, for example, to a research-based medical products company accustomed to marketing to individual, specialized physicians who make their own purchase decisions rather than to group practices or health care facilities where cost is a key consideration.

▲ For a company accustomed to moving at a measured pace, a segment characterized by frequent and rapid change or severe cyclical or seasonal fluctuations might be a poor fit. This situation applies, for example, to a company that makes luggage for business travelers and is considering making bookbags and the like for youngsters, whose tastes are highly changeable according to the latest fashion.

Differences between the company's current capabilities, experience, and traits and those needed to do business successfully in a new segment are manageable over time. Such differences don't necessarily mean that a segment should be set aside. But by recognizing the differences at this stage, you can avoid unrealistic expectations about early success with a minimal resource commitment.

Conclusions about attractiveness and fit can be added to the chart of customer segment distinctions as shown in Figure 1-7.

By assessing customer segments for profit potential, you have also identified any segment that is inherently unattractive and a poor fit with your company. When a segment with minimal profit potential is one that you currently serve, you can consider spreading the word inside the company to pay less attention to customers there, starting immediately. This may sound like a bold decision, but there is little to lose by merely filling orders if and when they come in from a low profit-potential segment, especially when company resources are constrained. Attention paid and resources committed to other segments will be more fruitful, contributing more to the company's profits and investment returns.

Knowing which customer segments offer good profit potential is important, but it is not enough to guide far-reaching decisions and near-term actions. Since success in a segment and the profits realized from it depend on how well you serve customers there, it's essential to understand their point of view in detail. Whether to explore a certain customer segment in depth depends mainly on the business issue you're using the CORe Method to address. Say you're setting out to maintain and improve profitability by anticipating changes in current customers' needs. In this instance, you'd explore any customer segment you currently serve that offers high profit potential where competition is strong or getting stronger. Whether you also explore a segment with medium potential is for you to judge.

Whatever the issue being addressed, you may unearth a highly attractive segment where the fit with the company's current capabilities is only so-so. This segment might be new to the company or one in which it has just a toehold. In-depth exploration will produce the information needed to determine what it would take for your company to become a leading supplier and whether you should enter or try to build a strong presence in that segment, based on realistic financial projections.

Figure 1-7. Customer segment attractiveness and fit: future profit potential.

Customer Segment	Distinctive Buying Factors	Customer Value Element Importance				Future Profit Potential	
		Product	Transac-tion	Support	Pricing	Inherent Attractiveness	Fit With Company Capabilities (Current)
Manufacturers/assemblers of automobiles, off-road equipment	Deliver to forecast, with some flexibility Large quantities of standard products (for current models only) Consistent product quality New model development support only Increasingly price/internal cost-conscious	M	H	M-L	M-H	L*	H
Large servicers of original equipment: fleet owners, car dealerships	Formulation/container size for current and older models, for specific makes Variable quantities hard to predict, hold limited inventory, immediate delivery of emergency orders Some technical problem solving	M	M-H	L	L	H	M
Aftermarket distributors	High, predictable volumes Ordering/shipping efficiency Quantities packaged for breakdown/retail sale Highly price-sensitive	L	H	L	M-H	H	M
Manufacturers/assemblers of custom engineered products for mining, civil engineering	Heavy product design support Job-dependent quantities Longer lead times acceptable but on-time delivery Pricing per job	H	L	H	L	L	H

*Though this segment's inherent attractiveness is low, it becomes medium as the entree to highly attractive segments, e.g., large servicers and aftermarket distributors.

Key: H = High, M = Medium, L = Low

▲   ▲   ▲

After defining customer segments relevant to your company, ascertaining those that offer the best profit potential, and selecting the segment or segments to be explored further, you now obtain firsthand knowledge of the customer perspective.

Part C: Customers' Viewpoint

In this part of Step One, you learn directly from customers what product and service attributes are most important in their purchase decisions, whom they consider their key suppliers, and how they view their suppliers' performance, including your company's. This can reveal customer needs that are currently unmet. You then outline with customers any other product or service innovations that would help meet their objectives. Part C is highlighted in Figure 1-8.

▲   ▲   ▲

The significance of knowledge garnered from customers cannot be overstated. This knowledge is the cornerstone of the foundation on which you'll base decisions on overall direction and develop the plan of action to pursue it. The principal use of information from customers is therefore to identify the changes your company needs to make to provide customers with outstanding value and the time and resources involved. You also use the customer perspective to evaluate key competitors.

Understanding the Customer Viewpoint in Depth

If you don't know what matters most to customers, the chances of your company's providing it are slim. Obvious as this may seem, few companies do a thorough job of finding out what drives customers' purchase decisions and what they are setting out to achieve. An organized effort reveals the opportunities to advance the company's standing with customers while minimizing the demand on their time.

Understanding the customer viewpoint in depth makes it

Figure 1-8. Step One—The Context: Understanding Customer Viewpoints, Part C.

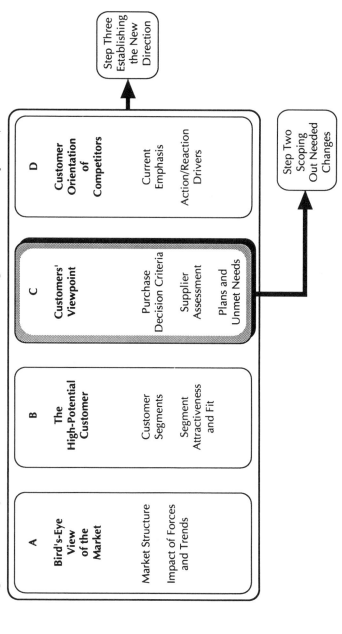

A

Bird's-Eye View of the Market

Market Structure

Impact of Forces and Trends

B

The High-Potential Customer

Customer Segments

Segment Attractiveness and Fit

C

Customers' Viewpoint

Purchase Decision Criteria

Supplier Assessment

Plans and Unmet Needs

D

Customer Orientation of Competitors

Current Emphasis

Action/Reaction Drivers

Step Three
Establishing the New Direction

Step Two
Scoping Out Needed Changes

possible to develop a plan of action that embodies customers' priorities, reflects key competitors' strengths and weaknesses, and ties in with the company's current capabilities, limitations, and objectives. Such an action plan is the shortest and surest path to realizing lasting improvement in financial performance.

Sophisticated customers make purchase decisions based on a set of product and service attributes that, as a whole, best meet their needs. It is this bundle of product and service attributes that provides value for customers. And it is delivering a superior value package that earns a company preferred supplier status with current customers and enables it to attract new ones. As a successful veteran salesman told a young colleague, "You're not selling a product. Our customers aren't deciding among products, they're deciding whom to buy from. From the customer's point of view, you're actually selling the company and what it can do for them."

In-depth understanding of the customers' perspective starts with their definitions, priorities, and measurable benchmarks for certain product and service attributes; examples are listed in Figure 1-9, grouped according to the four customer value elements. Earlier, in Part B, you used the relative importance of the value elements when defining customer segments. Here you find out firsthand how the customer perspective differs from segment to segment in terms of specific product and service attributes and their importance.

Many companies stipulate at length what's required to qualify as a supplier. Meeting these requirements can keep you on the list of approved suppliers, but the key to becoming or remaining a first-tier supplier is knowing the criteria that swing the purchase decision. Meeting these criteria can also make the difference between staying on the list and being dropped when customers reduce the number of suppliers they use.

Thus, whether or not you currently serve a particular customer segment, you need to know what matters most to customers there. This doesn't mean that your company should aim to provide everything that customers look for from the ideal supplier, but knowing what customers consider ideal will provide a frame of reference you can use to define the position your company will aim for. This will be as close as possible to the ideal, after determining

Figure 1-9. Customer value: a mix of product and service attributes.

Customer Value Element	Examples of Customer-Defined Product and Service Attributes
Product	In-use product characteristics Compatibility with current use procedures and manufacturing processes Customization, features, and options Consistent performance and reliability Package or container configuration Ease and safety of use, maintenance, handling, storage, disposal Parts compatibility Defect rate Shelf life
Transaction	Simplicity of ordering procedures and paperwork Informed sales reps and order processors Product availability dates Product line breadth Speedy credit clearance Prompt and/or on-time delivery Complete shipments and paperwork Responsiveness to customer schedule changes Shipment markings Clear and accurate invoices Responsiveness to questions about billing Timely resolution of shipping problems
Support	For customers who resell products: Provision of sales aids and point-of-purchase materials Co-op advertising and promotions Substantiated information on product advantages Customer sales training Product samples Administration of pull-through promotional programs For customers who use products: Installation assistance Maintenance service Product use training and problem solving Joint product development and pilot manufacture Easy-to-follow, accurate manuals and updates Regulatory assistance and advice on product disposal Spare parts and upgrades Products for trial use Advice on subsequent purchase of related products Assistance with efficiency improvements
Pricing	Absolute price levels and net price to customers after volume discounts and rebates or sales incentives No-cost replacement of lost or defective shipments Early advice on and frequency of changes in pricing and terms Warranty terms Acceptance of returned goods Billing terms and options Credit line flexibility Loan assistance

what's feasible with real-world internal limitations and what's desirable in terms of financial objectives.

Obtaining Key Customer Information Efficiently

Understanding the customer viewpoint in a segment calls for face-to-face interviews with one customer at a time according to a survey designed for that particular segment. Group discussion among people from several customer companies is not conducive to eliciting information about their inner workings and plans. Such topics are deemed inappropriate for discussion in the presence of representatives of competing companies.

There is no substitute for being on-site with the customer. Interviewing a customer at the customer's location lets you gauge reactions, probe, and observe in a way that's not possible with telephone interviews or written questionnaires (the latter are especially likely to have low response rates). But these days, many companies are inundated by suppliers' visits, telephone calls, questionnaires, and requests to participate in focus groups, in addition to regular sales calls. Your quest for information may be a nuisance to customers if you don't conduct it in an efficient and considerate manner. Prearranging your visits to suit customers' schedules shows that you appreciate the value of their time.

You need to meet the people who actually make purchase decisions, but being on-site makes it possible to talk with others who might be available on short notice. They could show you, for example, how your product is actually used and why they consider certain changes so important. You can see or hear for yourself how the results of your company's actions appear from the customers' perspective, such as poorly marked containers or a mismatch between invoices and the papers that accompany a shipment.

Conducting interviews segment by segment lets you limit the survey to a subset of customers within each segment. This subset must, however, be representative. Large established customers are obvious candidates to be interviewed, but the views of smaller customers that are gaining market share are especially significant. Their success indicates that they are doing an outstanding job of serving their customers—in ways that their competitors may have to emulate. By serving the emerging leaders effectively, you benefit from their success while anticipating the needs of the followers. Thus, a few companies—some established and some emerging, some that currently buy from you and some that don't—add up to a representative cross section of a customer segment.

The number of customers interviewed is less important than that they are representative. One company set out to interview fifteen customers in a segment made up of autonomous hotels and independent restaurants catering to wealthy local residents and traveling executives. After eight interviews, the survey showed clear patterns that were borne out in the remaining seven. Overly conscious of statistical significance and, therefore, doubting the validity of results from so limited a survey, the company elected to continue the interviews, raising the sample size to a hundred. The additional interviews produced the same conclusions as the initial ones. Carefully selecting the customers to be interviewed—as this company did with its original fifteen—produces valid results sooner and at lower cost.

The main purpose of customer interviews is to obtain new information. This information may, however, simply clarify, confirm, or refute deductions you've already made or put what you already know in a new context. Or what you learn may be a surprise or unflattering to your company. Dispassionate reactions help keep the spotlight where it belongs: on customers. A readiness and the ability to listen—to acknowledge and understand the customer's point of view—are crucial. Although it may be tempting to bring up subjects that are of greater interest to your company (its products, creative new marketing programs, successful improvement projects) than to customers, resisting this temptation shows people within the customer organization that you're genuinely interested in their views. As a result, they may be more willing to spend time and share information. And the interview stays on track to produce the information you set out to obtain.

Relative Importance of Product and Service Attributes. Open-ended questions based on predefined hypotheses show customers that you are informed about their business and let you get directly to the point: obtaining customer definitions and priorities for the various product and service attributes. Information developed earlier—about market forces and trends and about the customer segment—provides the basis for developing these hypotheses. Questions based on them might include:

- ▲ For distributors with nationwide scope: How do you need products packed for breakdown and shipment to their locations? In light of the volume of shipments you handle, how important are the simplicity of a supplier's paperwork and accuracy of billing?
- ▲ For manufacturers in a business where frequent product enhancements are the norm: How important is it for a supplier to keep up with your enhancements by making related revisions? How important are such revisions compared to further reduction in the defect levels of a supplier's current product configurations?
- ▲ For end users making repeat purchases of standard products: To what degree is an aspect of pricing (e.g., how volume discounts are structured, the frequency of price changes) an important consideration in purchase decisions?

Having an interview guide with such questions ensures consistency in the questions asked and how responses are recorded. And it makes compiling and interpreting the results easier and quicker. How tightly structured and detailed an interview guide needs to be depends primarily on how skilled the interviewers are and, to a degree, how knowledgeable they are about the industry. For experienced interviewers, the written guide can be relatively unstructured: They will shape the specific questions as the interview proceeds. Figure 1-10 shows an extract from a sample interview guide suitable for use by experienced interviewers. In this and other interview guide extracts, the company (interviewee) maintains and repairs transportation equipment parts.

Responses can be verified while on-site at the customer location. You can tell right away how much an attribute really matters by how customers track it. For example, when you hear that their benchmark for timely delivery is a certain number of days or weeks, and the person you're talking to has records at hand showing time from order placement to receipt, you can be sure that timely delivery is indeed highly important.

Figure 1-10. Sample interview guide: purchase decision criteria.

1. What criteria do you use to select among suppliers? (Examples for prompting: quality of workmanship, documentation, prompt estimates, turnaround time, range of maintenance capability, order status updates, slippage reporting, nonroutine repairs, problem solving, actual price vs. estimate)

2. What is the relative importance of each of these criteria? Do you expect their importance to change?

3. Which of these criteria do you have measurable benchmarks for? Which measurements do you take routinely? How often? What are your benchmarks for these criteria, measurable or otherwise?

4. Are any of these criteria assumed or givens? Which ones? Which swing the decision?

5. Which of the services your suppliers offer appeal to you the most? The least? (Verification question)

A chart displaying specific product and service attributes and their importance might look like that in Figure 1-11. (Such a chart would be compiled away from customers' premises and after several, if not all, interviews have been conducted.)

Key Suppliers' Performance. Customers' views on a supplier's competitors often differ from the view inside the supplier organization. Suppliers typically think of their competitors as companies that make the same products. Customers, however, buy a product to serve a particular purpose and may define your competitors more broadly to include those supplying different products that serve the same purpose. In the aviation aftermarket, for example, engine manufacturers make the bulk of their profits from the sale of new spare parts. Yet from the airlines' perspective, manufacturers of new parts compete with independent companies—and, in some instances, the airlines' own operations—that refurbish used parts—the very products the manufacturers want to replace.

Figure 1-11. Product and service attributes defined and weighted by customers.

Value Element	Product or Service Attribute	Importance		
		High	Medium	Low
Product	Product reliability*		■	
	Outer packaging strong enough to stack high on pallet (air conditioners 6 high)	■		
	Product that works out-of-box for 30 days		■	
	Spare parts packaged for forward shipment of one			■
Transaction	Product line breadth (single source for multiple appliances, full model range of each)		■	
	Reasonable pressure to take advantage of seasonal demand		■	
	Markings on unit shipping containers consistent with bill of lading	■		
	On-time receipt of precise order quantity	■		
	Speedy resolution of shipping problems			■
	Manufacturer-provided inventory management	■		
Support	National advertising	■		
	Attractive point-of-sale product information sheets		■	
	Response to peaks in demand (delivery within 48 hours)	■		
	Early notice of when product improvements take effect		■	
	Point-of-sale kit for forwarding to retailer			■
	Availability of spare parts			■
Pricing	Full truckload discounts regardless of product mix	■		
	Billing terms and conditions based on dollar volume (regardless of product mix) per time period (not per invoice)	■		
	Absolute price level to reflect responsibility for warranty fulfillment		■	
	Manufacturer responsible for lost shipments			■
	Credit for unfixable products			■
	Occasional flexibility on credit line		■	

Note: The company (interviewer) manufactures air conditioners. Customers (interviewees) distribute household appliances to retailers.

*End-use product performance characteristics are a given to distributors. Other givens include electrical standards and cost-price markups that are industry norms.

Therefore, from the customer perspective, you might be competing with the customer itself, another part of the customer company, or another part of your own company.

Having customers identify their key suppliers can provide vital new information. You might find that you've been targeting your marketing efforts against a company that isn't even mentioned. One company found that it had been reducing price to match a competitor whose overall performance ranked lower in customers' eyes. Customers may also know of potential new competitors: An overseas company or a local company seeking new opportunities may have been studying the market and conducting similar interviews. Furthermore, customers' views on the up-and-coming suppliers indicate where the toughest competition is likely to come from in the future.

A growing number of companies have formal systems to track their suppliers' performance. But even the views of less sophisticated and infrequent purchasers are significant. All purchasers judge from previous buying experiences, both their own and those of others they've heard about. Every purchase experience is likely to be stored away as part of a supplier's reputation.

As customers identify the top few suppliers, you might notice that a particular company is excluded. Finding out why can indicate practices and attitudes to avoid. For example, a customer might resent having to deal with several sales reps from the same company, each of whom is responsible for a separate product line. Or customers may perceive the technological leader to be arrogant and unresponsive.

Customers' assessments of a supplier's strength and weaknesses commonly differ from the supplier's views. From the supplier's viewpoint, what it has and is proud of comes to mind first, such as a leading-edge R&D program, nationwide service outlets, and state-of-the-art manufacturing. But customers judge a company on the basis of the products and services it provides and how well these meet their needs. Customers' views on your company's weaknesses may therefore be tough to swallow. But, you're only learning something that customers—and, probably, your more astute competitors—already know.

Sample questions to elicit customers' views on who the key suppliers are and how they assess the suppliers' performance are shown in Figure 1-12. Customers' assessments of supplier performance on highly important product and service attributes are most significant. It's possible that one of these represents a customer need that is not currently being met. For example, customers might be automating certain operations, but no supplier has yet revised its products and paperwork accordingly. An unmet need is an opportunity for your company, and one that competitors may not be aware of yet.

The supplier performance assessment can be added to the chart of the product and service attributes, as illustrated in Figure 1-13. It shows a considerable amount of information at a single glance. Again, the chart would be compiled away from customer premises after most of the interviews have been done. (How to use the information shown in this chart to evaluate competitors is described in Part D; how to use this information inside your company—to identify the changes it needs to make to advance its standing with customers—is described in Step Two.)

Figure 1-12. Sample interview guide: assessment of supplier performance.

---

1. Which suppliers do you consider the key ones? Which are likely to be the key suppliers in the future?

2. How does their performance compare with your decision criteria? Why do you rank each supplier this way?

3. Which of these suppliers would you consider using? Why? Which of these suppliers would you *not* consider using? Why not?

4. Do you provide your suppliers with information on their performance? Do they act on this information?

5. Which suppliers do you currently use? Have you used? What improvements are you looking for from your current suppliers?

6. Does any supplier meet all your decision criteria? Which suppliers come closest?

Figure 1-13. Customer assessment of four suppliers' performances.

Attributes *Highly Important to Customers*	Customers' Supplier Ranking			
	1	*2*	*3*	*4*
Outer packaging strong enough to stack high on pallet (air conditioners 6 high)	Co. D	Co. A	Co. B	Co. C
On-time receipt of precise order quantity	Co. A	Co. B	Co. D	Co. C
Manufacturer-provided inventory management	Co. B	Co. A	Co. C	Co. D
National advertising	Co. A	Co. B	Co. C	Co. D
Response to peaks in demand (delivery within 48 hours)	Co. B	Co. D	Co. A	Co. C
Full truckload discounts regardless of product mix	Co. C	Co. A	Co. B	Co. D
Billing terms and conditions based on dollar volume per time period	Co. C	Co. A	Co. D	Co. B

Product and Service Innovations. The last topic for the interviews is product and service innovations that would support customers' key objectives and initiatives. You may have already learned of customers' current needs that are unmet. In addition, customers probably have projects under way or in the planning stage. What any up-and-coming customer company—one that's currently gaining market share from its competitors—is setting out to do warrants particularly close attention.

Whether customers' initiatives are to enhance revenue or reduce costs, you can probably support them in some way. For example, a customer that is expanding into a new market or developing new products might appreciate technical assistance with product development as well as related revisions to your products. And a customer streamlining its operations might appreciate your performing incoming quality control before shipping the product or your holding inventory for it to draw from. Sample questions to prompt discussion about customers' plans are shown in Figure 1-14.

What comes up in discussion with customers about innovations may or may not be new to you. You might already have on the drawing board a product allowing customers to combine several operations, be considering a package configuration that would simplify customers' materials handling, or be working on a way to transmit information electronically. More important is knowing which products or services your company is currently developing or considering actually tie in with customers' needs. Equally

Figure 1-14. Sample interview guide: plans and problems.

---

1. Do you plan to do more or less maintenance work for yourself in the future? If so, what type of work will you increase or decrease? Why?

2. Are you contemplating changing your suppliers? If so, why and how soon?

3. What initiatives or problems are you currently working on or considering working on? How could a supplier assist you with these?

---

important is finding out about a need for innovations you hadn't thought of yet.

Customers may have needs that tie in with abilities your company has but that hadn't been seen as a way to add to value for customers. For example, one company found that customers were grappling with a particular operational improvement program despite copious assistance from outside specialists. The company had implemented such a program itself and knew firsthand what was involved. Another company found that its customers had equipment representing a considerable investment standing idle because it needed an unusual repair that the company's technical problem solvers might be able to accomplish. The know-how of people at your company could be of value to customers in terms of their objectives and problems and offers an innovative way to serve them that your competitors may not be able to match.

▲   ▲   ▲

Having learned from customers the product and service attributes that matter most, who they think the key suppliers are, and their views of supplier performance, and having gained insight into customers' plans, you now use this information in two ways: to evaluate competitors and to direct the internal investigation. Here, the CORe Method takes parallel paths, as shown in Figure 1-1. To make the earliest possible use of what has been learned so far, you proceed to Step Two—Concreteness: Scoping Out Needed Changes, while completing Part D of Step One.

Part D: Customer Orientation of Competitors

In the last part of Step One you evaluate key competitors to determine the probable impact of their current actions on their performance and what their future actions are likely to be. You also identify what is likely to drive competitors' reactions to actions taken by other suppliers. Part D is highlighted in Figure 1-15.

▲   ▲   ▲

Customers must be the focal point and principal consider-

Figure 1-15. Step One—The Context: Understanding Customer Viewpoints, Part D.

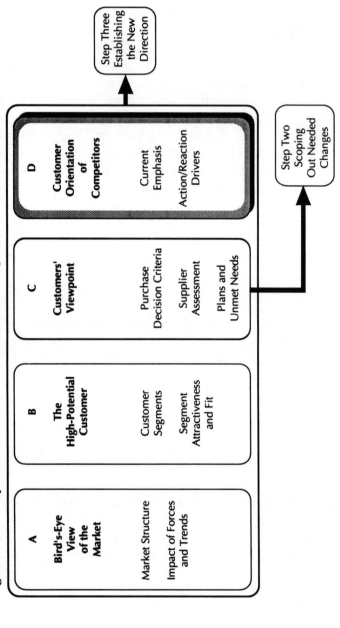

ation. However, what your competitors do can influence the effectiveness of the actions your company will take. Improvement efforts that competitors are working on today will affect how well they serve customers. Insight into the probable impact of these efforts, and into competitors' likely actions, therefore helps ensure that the direction you decide on doesn't become outdated. And discerning the probable source and nature of reactions to your actions lets you consider ahead of time whether and how to counter any retaliation.

Assessing the Competition

Knowing from customers who they think your competitors are and might be, and how customers assess their performance, gives you a head start on competitive analysis, but you do need to select which competitors to analyze. Concentrate on those whose performance currently ranks highest with customers in the segment being explored and perhaps a few other competing suppliers. These might be ones that customers don't yet consider among the top few but whose performance is improving significantly, or companies that you think might enter the market.

When customers have identified top-rated suppliers that you never considered to be competitors, you may need to collect basic information on them. Sources of information include trade magazines, general business publications, the competitors' annual reports and 10Ks, and government reports. Such sources provide background data and statistics such as company size; other business lines and their financial significance; technology, both in-house and through relationships with research organizations or other companies; whether the competitor is independent or a subsidiary and, if a subsidiary, its degree of autonomy; locations, including manufacturing, sales, service, and distribution sites; key executives and their backgrounds; and uses of funds. More up-to-date and detailed information can come from local newspapers; marketing materials and products; advertisements for job openings; recent filings with government departments, such as patent applications; and discussions at trade shows. It was during such a discussion that one company making components for use in capital equipment found out that a key competitor had manufacturing capabilities that the company lacked and had to subcontract for. This explained how the competitor could consistently deliver so promptly.

What appears at first to be a competitor's advantage can, on closer examination, be a vulnerability that impedes its ability to serve customers. For example, smaller companies with fewer layers of management are commonly thought to have a favorable cost structure and greater flexibility. But in its quest for lowest-cost status, such a company might be taking risky regulatory or environmental shortcuts, which, if discovered, could interrupt its product supply. The subsidiary of a large corporation may appear to have an advantage in its access to financial resources. But when the parent company emphasizes centralized authority or mandates the improvement approaches and other activities to be pursued, it can unwittingly take the subsidiary's attention away from its customers and its prompt response to changes in their needs.

Studying a competitor's products can uncover crucial information. The use of certain materials and simpler manufacturing processes can explain how a competitor affords lower prices. Certain aspects of product design can explain specific performance characteristics. Conversations at technical conferences and management seminars can provide useful insight into competitors' initiatives, such as development of a new product or adoption of a new production planning methodology.

These scraps of information have to be verified and sifted. People at your company—especially in the sales force and field service—and industry and government experts can augment, confirm, or refute information gleaned from other sources. Once confirmed, information about competitors' activities must be screened to determine its relevance to customers and, therefore, to your company.

In-depth knowledge of the customer perspective gained in Part C provides a framework to evaluate competitors' actions and to guide the search for additional relevant information. It may be interesting to know that a competitor is relocating its headquarters, but this is unlikely to affect the way it serves its customers. The product and service attributes that matter most to customers determine the significance of competing companies' current initiatives. These attributes can be identified from the results of customer interviews, as shown in a chart such as that in Figure 1-11. For example, if turnaround time is important to customers, but a competitor is concentrating on cost reductions, this is an opportunity for your company to gain market share. But a company that is building manufacturing or distribution facilities on customers' doorsteps is going to be hard to beat.

Actions that do tie in with customers' priorities suggest that a competitor is well-informed about its customers' needs. However, this tie-in might be fortuitous. A competitor beefing up its capability to provide product support, rather than relying on third parties to do so, might be responding to customer needs or it may be merely forward integrating in the quest for wider margins.

More important than the reason behind a competitor's actions is whether they affect value provided to customers. A competitor's efforts may actually detract from customer value. For example, if customers want to be able to talk to a person on the telephone for information or advice, a competitor's new answering system that has preset options for callers or requires that they leave a message for callback can cause customers to call another supplier. The probable impact of a competitor's actions on its standing with customers can be noted on a chart such as that shown in Figure 1-16. Innovations that competitors are working on can also be evaluated from the customer perspective to determine whether they represent a real benefit and, therefore, whether these innovations are significant to your company.

Predicting Competitors' Future Actions and Reactions

A competing company's roots and the background of its key executives are usually the strongest determinants of its future actions and reactions. Organizations and individuals tend to rely on what worked for them in the past. A research-based company is likely to continue investing in new products for sale at premium prices. A high-volume, low-cost producer of standard products is likely to emphasize price, shying away from more radical actions such as offering customization. And a general manager whose

Figure 1-16. Probable changes in competitors' performance.

Attributes Highly Important to Customers	Customers' Supplier Ranking			
	1	2	3	4
Outer packaging strong enough to stack high on pallet (air conditioners 6 high)	Co. D	Co. A	Co. B	Co. C
On-time receipt of precise order quantity	Co. A	Co. B	Co. D → Co. C	Co. C
Manufacturer-provided inventory management	Co. B	Co. A ↓	Co. C	Co. D
National advertising	Co. A	Co. B	Co. C → Co. D	Co. D
Response to peaks in demand (delivery within 48 hours)	Co. B	Co. D ↑	Co. A	Co. C
Full truckload discounts regardless of product mix	Co. C	Co. A	Co. B	Co. D
Billing terms and conditions based on dollar volume per time period	Co. C	Co. A	Co. D	Co. B

background is in sales or marketing is likely to step up selling, advertising, and promotional efforts.

Whether a competitor reacts to another supplier's actions depends largely on the importance of the particular business and on the competitor's own plans and problems. At some companies, where a certain type of customer or product line represents a significant portion of revenue, any move made by a competing supplier elicits a response. Other companies tend to wait and see and react only to major competitive actions.

Whatever a competitor's predisposition to retaliation, all companies have their own priorities to attend to, which can delay a reaction. A new product launch, a recent reorganization, a disagreement with a key customer, overseas expansion, the assimilation of an acquisition, a labor problem, and financial difficulties can all take a competitor's attention away from other suppliers and, therefore, from what your company is doing.

Major changes inside a competing company can signal a shift in its approach to the market. Organizational changes are key indicators, implying a change in emphasis on certain market areas, greater orientation toward customers, or a more aggressive attitude toward competition. A change in organizational structure, such as having a business unit report directly to the CEO, can indicate added emphasis on a customer segment that's significant to your company. The arrival or promotion of key executives, such as when a company is taken over or current management retires, can imply a more activist role for the competitor and a shift in its emphasis from, say, sales to finance or from operations to marketing.

Changes in how a competitor commits resources can also indicate a change in its direction. How soon these changes might have an impact varies. For instance, increased investment in an R&D program might take years to bear fruit; an agreement with another company to market its current products, or a major sales force expansion, is likely to have an earlier impact.

Continuous monitoring of competitors' actions will reveal such changes as they occur. By reviewing a change in light of customers' priorities, you can identify the likely impact on the competitor's standing with customers and what, if anything, the change means for your company.

▲   ▲   ▲

Having assessed key competitors' current and probable actions from the viewpoint of customers in a segment or segments
you're analyzing, and having gained insight into how likely a
particular competitor is to retaliate, you have completed the last
part of Step One.

Figure 1-17. Step One—The Context: Understanding Customer Viewpoints, recap.

Part	What You Achieved and How
A Bird's-Eye View of the Market	Determined what lies ahead for customers and your company by: ▲ Developing an overview of the market structure ▲ Interpreting market forces and trends
B The High-Potential Customer	Specified a market area or areas with the profit potential to be analyzed in depth by: ▲ Segmenting the market according to factors distinguishing customer buying practices ▲ Assessing customer segments for inherent attractiveness and fit with the company's current capabilities and roots
C Customers' Viewpoint	Uncovered the product and service attributes that carry the greatest weight in customers' purchase decisions, their assessment of key suppliers' perfor- mance, and the innovations of real benefit to them by: ▲ Selecting a representative subset of customers in a specific segment ▲ Preparing hypotheses and an interview guide ▲ Conducting in-person interviews at customer locations
D Customer Orientation of Competitors	Determined the likely changes in principal competi- tors' performance and their likely actions by: ▲ Evaluating competitors' improvement efforts from the customer viewpoint ▲ Identifying the probable drivers of competitors' future actions and reactions

The intelligence gathered here is not, by itself, the basis for decisions. The competitive situation now and in the foreseeable future is just one consideration in defining direction and priorities. Other key considerations are the attractiveness of a customer segment, what the customers in that segment are seeking, and the level of performance that your company can realistically attain, given time and resource limitations. How to determine the internal changes needed to provide the product and services that matter most to customers is described in Step Two.

Recap of Step One—The Context

In Step One—The Context, you found out from customers in a segment with significant profit potential which product and service attributes matter most to them and what they consider their suppliers' strengths and weaknesses. You then used the information from customers to evaluate key competitors.

Having up-to-date facts on customer prospects and views will make it possible to:

▲ Define the internal changes needed to become or remain a leading supplier; and
▲ Determine which changes will make the most of the company's current strengths and resources and produce higher profits and investment returns.

Figure 1-17 summarizes what was done in Step One.

Step Two

Concreteness: Scoping Out Needed Changes

In Step Two, you evaluate your company from the customer perspective to identify the changes that will advance its performance and then gauge the time and resources required. Based on this outside-in view of the company, the evaluation crosses internal boundaries to concentrate on the areas that together sway delivery of certain product and service attributes. People from various departments who know firsthand how each part of the organization operates make up teams that work in parallel.

Using the customer viewpoint to focus the internal investigation produces information complementary to that obtained about the market, customers, and competitors. The result is a cohesive foundation on which to base decisions on direction and to shape a plan of action. Broad involvement in the investigation spreads awareness of customers and of the need for change. It also engenders a sense of ownership among people who will work on or be affected by implementation.

▲　　▲　　▲

Step Two has four parts:

Part A Company Skills to Look Into
Part B Needed Changes and Ways to Make Them
Part C Practical Matters—Actions, Timing, and Resources
Part D Consolidated Findings

The contents of this step and how it connects with the others are shown in Figure 2-1.

Figure 2-1. Step Two—Concreteness: Scoping Out Needed Changes.

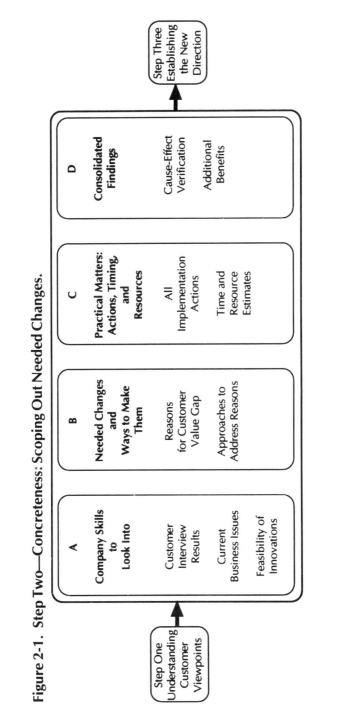

Step One
Understanding
Customer
Viewpoints

A

**Company Skills
to
Look Into**

Customer
Interview
Results

Current
Business Issues

Feasibility of
Innovations

B

**Needed Changes
and
Ways to Make
Them**

Reasons
for Customer
Value Gap

Approaches to
Address Reasons

C

**Practical Matters:
Actions, Timing,
and
Resources**

All
Implementation
Actions

Time and
Resource
Estimates

D

**Consolidated
Findings**

Cause-Effect
Verification

Additional
Benefits

Step Three
Establishing
the New
Direction

Working through Step Two provides information and insight to answer key questions about your company's capabilities, how best to develop them, and the changes and actions that would be most fruitful. For example:

▲ How can we supply our product the way customers want it (in bulk, with more or fewer features and options, customized)? Do we have the equipment needed? If not, what would it cost? How much training would be required? How long would it take before we could begin shipping?

▲ What are the best ways to speed product delivery—dramatically? Who would need to be involved? How much reduction can we realistically expect, and how soon? What cost decrease might we also expect as a result?

▲ What impact will this proposed product revision have on how we currently manufacture, test, store, and ship products and provide field service?

▲ Certain products and customers seem to take a disproportionate amount of . . . (technical support, selling effort, marketing funds), which isn't reflected in the standard cost or pricing for these products or customers. How profitable are they really?

▲ Demand through mail order is growing fast. What do we need to do to take advantage of this? Which departments would be involved? How much of their time would be needed to set up this type of business and stay on top of it?

▲ Handling customers' calls for technical problem solving, some of which are complaints, currently involves mountains of paperwork and many hours in technical service, quality assurance, manufacturing, and marketing. How can we respond sooner—and more economically—to these calls?

▲ Is this equipment, or other investment, really necessary? Are there other ways to . . . (increase flexibility, enhance capabilities, increase capacity) with a lower investment—or none at all?

▲ One of our competitors has facilities close to our customers. How might we provide the same level of service? If we choose to provide local storage or production, should we lease space, buy a facility, or build? Could we get the same result by shipping directly to end users? By holding inventory for customers to draw from as needed?

▲ We're already reducing labor content successfully and using less expensive materials wherever we can without jeopardizing product performance. How do we get a handle on overhead costs without jeopardizing service to customers?

▲ Customers claim that we have difficulty providing spare parts quickly. How can we cut the time to deliver spares? How can we prevent them, and custom products, from upsetting supply of other products?

The Key to Attainable Targets: Knowing Implementation Requirements

For most companies, Step Two of the CORe Method represents a major departure from customary decision-making practice. The fundamental difference is this: Instead of making decisions based on information about the market and customers and then collecting information on implementation, you identify implementation requirements first. Decisions are made later. The experience of two companies illustrates the pitfalls inherent in the customary decisions-first sequence:

One company saw an opportunity in a new market area, projected results (market share, revenue, and profits), and started selling there. Eighteen months later, the company had obtained some new business but had achieved only a small fraction of the projected profit.

Another company decided that an intense product development effort was the way to overtake competition in a critical current market. The required engineering resources were planned and budgeted. But demands on manufacturing (to gear up production and then climb the learning curve) as well as on marketing and sales (for sales training, advertising, initial customer support, service manuals, and so on) drove the company to a loss position.

In both instances, the decision on whether, and possibly how, to proceed would have been different had management known in advance what implementation would entail.

Another way of seeing the distinction between customary practice and the CORe Method is in terms of setting objectives. Usually managers start with an objective (e.g., to realize a certain revenue, introduce a new product, achieve a certain level of customer satisfaction, penetrate another market area) and then figure out what it would take to accomplish that objective. With the CORe Method, this sequence is reversed. First you find out what it will take for your company to provide the key product and service attributes customers seek, and then you use this information to set direction and actual objectives. This way, you have good reason to believe that target levels of performance—for customers and financial results—are indeed attainable.

Determining the time and resources required to provide superior value to customers *before* setting direction, planning action, and allocating resources therefore avoids an exercise that is disappointing, frustrating, time-consuming, and often unsuccessful. Scoping out needed changes at this stage also produces more accurate estimates of time and cost. Estimates generated after a high-level decision tend to reflect what management is thought to want to hear—namely, that the decision makes sense. This is likely to produce understated estimates, meaning that the basis of the financial projection is perilously flawed. Alternatively, estimates based on fear of failure are likely to be overstated, since the status quo is perceived as less risky than change.

Building a strong foundation for your decision making is the thrust of Step Two—Concreteness, which reveals what it will take for your company to achieve a stronger position in a customer segment currently served or to establish a strong position in another segment.

Part A: Company Skills to Look Into

The business unit management team uses information from and about customers to define the scope of the internal investigation. The product and service attributes to be investigated are specified, taking into consideration the issue you set out to address, the possibility that advancing the company's performance in one customer segment would strengthen it in another and the feasibility of innovations. Part A is highlighted in Figure 2-2.

▲ ▲ ▲

The higher up one is in the organization, the easier it is to lose touch with the details of day-to-day activities and the multiple interactions that add up to delivering products and providing services to customers. Rarely can the head of any one functional area know enough about the other areas to speak for them accurately. Thus, the people best qualified to define what's involved in serving customers more effectively are at lower levels and in various parts of the organization. These people need guidance before the investigation can start.

Stipulation by senior management of the product and service attributes to be investigated also focuses these people's efforts directly on producing the key information needed, so you won't have to plow through and make sense of an exhaustive review. Tight focus also avoids tying up an army of people in analyzing areas and activities of little significance to customers or that have little bearing on profitability.

Concentrating on Company Abilities, Not Assets

Standing in the customers' shoes makes it possible to see the company or business unit from a new vantage point—from the outside in. Since customers view a company's capabilities in terms of its overall effectiveness—its ability to deliver value—their vantage point puts the emphasis on what the company can do rather than on what it has.

From the traditional viewpoint inside the company, its capabilities are viewed in terms of assets and resources. But these don't matter to customers. More significant to customers is how these assets and resources translate into products and services that effectively differentiate a company from its competitors. What a company considers a source of *competitive* advantage is often a source of pride, but does little for company profits if it doesn't

Figure 2-2. Step Two—Concreteness: Scoping Out Needed Changes, Part A.

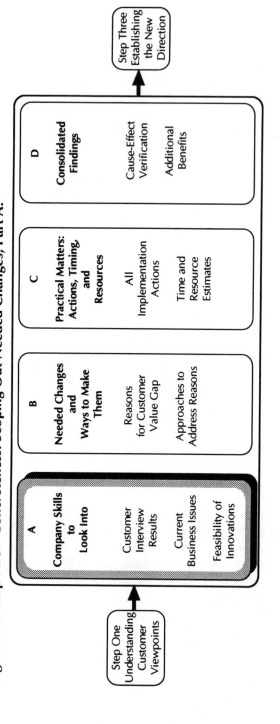

Step One
Understanding
Customer
Viewpoints

A

**Company Skills
to
Look Into**

Customer
Interview
Results

Current
Business Issues

Feasibility of
Innovations

B

**Needed Changes
and
Ways to Make
Them**

Reasons
for Customer
Value Gap

Approaches to
Address Reasons

C

**Practical Matters:
Actions, Timing,
and
Resources**

All
Implementation
Actions

Time and
Resource
Estimates

D

**Consolidated
Findings**

Cause-Effect
Verification

Additional
Benefits

Step Three
Establishing
the New
Direction

produce *advantage for customers.* Moreover, other companies have access to the same or equivalent equipment and technology and to the same pool of human talent.

Some assets and resources are viewed as belonging to the company as a whole (brand names, proprietary technology, land, cash). And, others (broad sales coverage, a leading-edge R&D program, sophisticated manufacturing processes) are viewed as "belonging" to certain parts of the organization. But internal jurisdictions are also irrelevant to customers and should be invisible to them. Parochialism shortchanges the organization as a whole, such as when customers hear "It's not *my* job" or "We can't do . . . because *they.* . . ." And internally defined capabilities—assets and resources accumulated in the past—aren't necessarily a strength when serving customers now and in the future.

As revealed in Step One, The Context: Understanding Customer Viewpoints, different types of customers define value differently. This means that what the company sees as a strength may or may not be one in a particular customer segment. For example, product line breadth is often considered by a company to be a strength. But for customers who pick among several suppliers' products, a company's product line breadth is of little significance.

Seeing the company from the customer perspective can open up new avenues to build on its true strengths and profit from them. For example, when product line breadth *is* significant to customers, broadening it further by reselling other manufacturers' products would be of greater benefit to customers than adding bells and whistles to current products. And when your customers are adopting new ways to develop their business and attract new customers, making your marketing and technical expertise available to support these efforts would be more productive than selling more aggressively or eliminating the last drop of inefficiency from internal activities.

Focusing the Internal Analysis

The value elements that are critical to customers indicate where to focus the investigation. Each customer value element corresponds to a company capability to which various parts of the organization contribute. The company's performance—its overall ability to deliver value to customers—is made up of four capabilities, which correspond to the four customer value elements. Figure 2-3 shows the company capability that each customer value element relates to.

Reviewing the product and service attributes weighted highly by customers reveals a value element that's critical in a specific segment. For example, in one customer segment, purchase decisions may hinge on speedy order processing and frequent shipment of partial order quantities, meaning that the Transaction is the key value element. In another segment, aspects of the Product, such as customization, easy-to-open packaging, or low defect levels, might be more important. (The customer value elements into which specific product and service attributes fall were shown in Figure 1-9 in Step One.) The number of investigating teams depends on the number of value elements you elect to analyze.

Any highly important product or service attribute on which customers have identified your company's performance as weak or for which their need is unmet is a prime candidate for inclusion in the investigation. For example, if customers' decisions among suppliers hinge on a certain level of product quality, which your company currently provides, followed by ease-of-use characteristics and product-use assistance, where your performance falls

Figure 2-3. The customer value–company performance connection.

Customer Value Element	Capability Driving Company Performance
Product	Product design and manufacturing processes
Transaction	Flows of product information and manufacturing materials
Support	Deployment of expertise (marketing, technical, etc.) and availability of supplies or materials
Pricing	Policies and cost structure

short, Product and Support should be the focal points of your investigation. This doesn't mean that manufacturing quality, delivery, and pricing are unimportant, only that improving them would have less impact.

The company capabilities you investigate when using the CORe Method are likely to differ from those emphasized in the past. For example, at a company that custom-packages consumer products for mass marketers, the customer viewpoint revealed that an outstanding product was not enough. Important product characteristics (e.g., better taste, greater safety) had enabled this company to become an established supplier, but becoming a preferred supplier required that it meet other criteria. The mass marketers' (customers') views are shown in Figure 2-4, in which Company D represents this company. Each of Company D's competitors has its particular strength (Company A, Support; B, Pricing; C, Transaction), but D does not, having assumed that the combination of its superior product and reasonable pricing was enough. What Company D hadn't realized was the importance to customers of nonproduct, nonprice attributes. Nor had it known what these attributes were. For Company D, therefore, the customer value elements to investigate are Support (attributes 1 and 4 in the figure) and the Transaction (attributes 2, 3, and 5). Since the customer value gap involves two elements, two investigating teams are needed.

In addition to being used to define the scope of analysis in Step Two, information from customers can be put to immediate use for other purposes. For example, once customers become familiar with a product or have developed the requisite expertise in-house, they no longer value as highly the company-provided product-use support. Deemphasizing this type of support for these customers would free resources for more productive activities. And having up-to-date information from customers lets you take a fresh look at your marketing materials to verify that the messages they convey tie in with what matters to customers and what they see as the company's strengths.

Considering Your Business Issue

Which product and service attributes to investigate also depends on the issue you set out to address. A producer of industrial

Figure 2-4. Customer assessment of suppliers' performances.

Customer Value Element	Product and Service Attributes Rated Highly Important by Customers	Customers' Supplier Ranking			
		1	2	3	4
Support	1. Responsiveness to requests for packaging and copy changes	Co. A	Co. C	Co. B	Co. D
Transaction	2. Delivery by the time agreed to	Co. C	Co. A	Co. D	Co. B
Transaction	3. Copy of product test results with shipment (within 24 hours at the latest)	Co. C	Co. A	Co. B	Co. D
Support	4. Early notice of product revisions initiated by the supplier	Co. A	Co. B	Co. C	Co. D
Transaction	5. Full production records within a week after shipment receipt	Co. B	Co. C	Co. D	Co. A
Pricing	6. Net pricing to allow 40 percent markup	Co. B	Co. D	Co. A	Co. C

chemicals, considering the issue of whether to continue funding a particular R&D project, found that its sophisticated new metering device had appeal only in a customer segment that, though sizable, offered only so-so growth. Product use in this segment would be limited to special applications requiring preset quantities within a narrow range. This meant that potential demand for the new device was insufficient to warrant continued development. The decision was made to abandon the project.

However, the same customer segment was looking for a product configured in such a way that the amount used could be varied. The company could provide this configuration by reformulating an existing product and packaging it in reclosable containers of a type used for another product. This idea had been around for some time, but it had not been pursued for lack of hard information on its relevance to customers. Knowing what was involved in providing this product would make it possible to determine its likely impact on profits, meaning that investigation of the Product was called for.

Other types of issues are less clear-cut, such as maintaining or strengthening a company's standing to improve profitability. A division of a large corporation—a business unit supplying customized components for temperature-control systems—was losing market share in the customer segment that represented its core business. The loss of share was happening despite generous marketing expenditures and price reductions. Margins were shrinking as manufacturing cost reductions lagged behind price decreases. Yet price was a relatively minor consideration in customers' purchase decisions. Attributes related to the Product and Support carried greater weight. In fact, customers were willing to pay premium prices for a product with measurably superior performance (longer-lasting parts, higher energy efficiency) that was designed to meet their needs with the help of the manufacturers' engineers. And the division excelled in Product and Support.

What had caused customers to turn to the division's competitors—and forgo a superior product—was its inability to deliver as agreed. In this customer segment, prompt delivery was not the point, on-time delivery was. Orders were placed, terms were established, and specifications were defined months ahead of time; yet, the division missed due date after due date. Fixing the delivery problem would allow it to regain lost customers, return to premium pricing, and possibly cut back on marketing expenses. This promised a surer way to raise profitability in the core business up to, and probably above, former levels than would increasing the pressure to reduce manufacturing costs.

Strengthening a company's ability to serve customers in one segment can also be of benefit in another. The results of customer interviews conducted in different segments indicate whether this ideal situation applies. The division making temperature-control components found that its product's performance characteristics had value to end users in a relatively new segment for the division, one in which customers use standard products and order in large quantities. In this segment, lead times are measured in weeks, and prompt and unerring delivery is crucial. Late or incomplete shipments shut down customers' assembly lines. Thus, the division's inability to deliver would completely derail its efforts to penetrate this segment. But building its capability related to the Transaction would be of benefit in the core business as well as in this newer, higher-growth customer segment. And since customers in the newer segment seek a similar product (differing only in size and lack of customization), developing and producing that product was within the division's current design and manufacturing capability.

Whether a product or service innovation is realistic for your company is a matter of judgment. Some innovations are more desirable than feasible. For example, when customers seek assistance in inventory management and only one other supplier provides support of this kind, it's obviously desirable to do so too. But if production planning and inventory control are areas in which your company is less than expert, setting out to help customers manage their inventory would be overly ambitious. Acknowledging limitations can be disquieting, but it avoids sending an investigating team on a wild-goose chase. Making such determinations calls for deep knowledge of a range of functional areas.

Involving Senior People From All Functional Areas

Tapping the expertise of people in several functional areas at this stage may be a departure from standard practice, but it is essential. At most companies, the key players in discussions about product development are marketing and R&D, with consultation with the general manager and help from finance to run the numbers. Entering or penetrating a new market area is typically a subject for sales and marketing, again with the general manager.

Such limited participation glosses over the indisputable fact that success depends on the combined effort of all the parts of the organization that work on supplying the products and providing service to customers, such as manufacturing and quality assurance, production planning and purchasing, order processing and shipping, billing, and technical service. Thus, having all functions represented when determining which product and service attributes to investigate avoids dangerous assumptions and brings real-world considerations to the fore.

Eliciting the views of all functions indicates whether in-depth exploration of an innovation is likely to be worthwhile. These views might bring to light, for example, the fact that:

▲ Revising a product to provide attributes sought by customers is technologically feasible.
▲ Manufacturing the revised product would call for reconfiguring equipment in such a way as to make it unsuitable for other products.
▲ Use of the materials envisaged would be subject to a recently issued regulatory ruling.

The management team aware of such factors can use its collective judgment to determine whether to include an innovation in the investigation.

It's also up to the management team's collective judgment whether exploring ways to lower costs for internal reasons is warranted and realistic in terms of the current work load. All companies are concerned about lowering costs, but if the Pricing topics that affect customers (e.g., volume discounts, sales incentive rebates, payment terms) are not among the product and service attributes specified so far, you would not have a team investigating Pricing. However, you might see a need to look into the costs of serving a certain customer segment to get a truer picture of where bottom-line profits are being generated. Or, now that you know what matters most to customers, you could use this information to determine where costs might be reduced without ill effects.

Since the investigation touches all functional areas in depth, the people working on it need to understand its significance. The fact that the heads of all functions participated in defining the scope makes it clear that the investigation is for the organization as a whole, not just for one or two areas or people. Explaining that the purpose is to determine what's needed to enable the company to become or remain a leading supplier makes it easy for people to understand the importance of the investigation. This gets the investigating teams off to a good start. As they proceed, management will need to be in touch occasionally to provide guidance and to hear what the teams are finding. Management's interest and willingness to listen will help maintain the momentum.

▲   ▲   ▲

Once the management team has defined the scope of the investigation in light of customers' priorities, current business issues, and the company's limitations, identification of the changes needed to close the performance gap begins.

Part B: Needed Changes and Ways to Make Them

Each investigating team proposes ways to close the gap between what customers seek and the product or service attributes the company can currently provide. They start by locating the activities, practices, and resource capabilities associated with a certain gap and tracing its origins. Based on these origins, the teams define approaches to close the gap. Part B is highlighted in Figure 2-5.

▲   ▲   ▲

Failure to identify the underlying reasons for company performance that is at variance with customers' needs and priorities risks pursuing changes that are at best partially effective. Band-aid measures, which cure symptoms but not causes, are one danger. Another is localized remedies that can, in the worst case, do more harm than good. But identifying the underlying reasons for the gap between value sought and value provided makes it possible to

Figure 2-5. Step Two—Concreteness: Scoping Out Needed Changes, Part B.

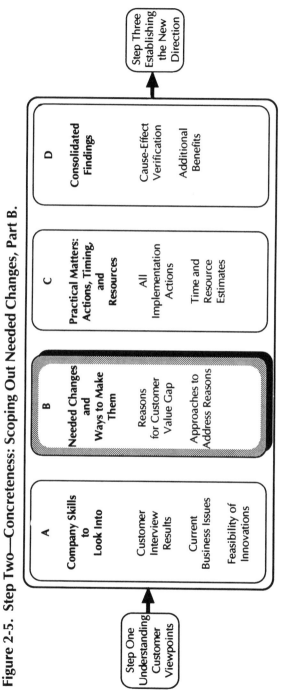

Step One
Understanding
Customer
Viewpoints

A

Company Skills to Look Into

Customer Interview Results

Current Business Issues

Feasibility of Innovations

B

Needed Changes and Ways to Make Them

Reasons for Customer Value Gap

Approaches to Address Reasons

C

Practical Matters: Actions, Timing, and Resources

All Implementation Actions

Time and Resource Estimates

D

Consolidated Findings

Cause-Effect Verification

Additional Benefits

Step Three
Establishing the New Direction

define a customized improvement program. These tailor-made changes will enable a company to provide superior value in the shortest possible time with a minimum of disruption and the lowest possible resource commitment.

Focusing on Reality

Internal analysis is not a witch-hunt to assign blame; its purposes are positive. However, getting into the inner workings of an organization is potentially sensitive. Some people welcome attention and the chance to voice their suggestions; others may resent or feel threatened by someone looking over their shoulders. Involving people in defining the ways to accomplish needed changes lets them see at the outset that they are perceived as part of the solution, not the cause of the problem.

Seeing the company as a whole from the outside, as customers do, ensures consideration of each function's and department's contribution and the key interactions among them.

The investigating teams work in parallel, each concentrating on one company capability and the topics it encompasses. These are shown in Figure 2-6. You'll notice the absence of any reference to where responsibility lies, as department names would imply. These are irrelevant. The objective for each team is to compare in a constructive way how things actually are (not how they are supposed to be or thought to be) with how they need to be in order to deliver value for customers.

Starting with reality leads directly to identification of the root causes of a customer value gap, leading to faster definition of the approaches to effect needed changes. You don't need to train people in elaborate problem-analysis techniques, the use of which can be unnecessarily time-consuming. The people charged with defining needed changes—those who work directly on delivering value to customers day to day—may already know, for example, which procedures keep product information from getting into sales reps' hands for speedy response to customers' questions, or where use of old tooling or certain materials affects product quality and generates scrap.

Tapping these people's firsthand knowledge avoids spending time on, for example, hypothesizing about possible causes and

Figure 2-6. Topics encompassed by a company capability.

Customer Value Element	Company Capability	Examples of Topics
Product	Product design and manufacturing processes	Product and package configuration and labeling; raw materials procurement, manufacturing instructions and equipment, quality assurance methods
Transaction	Flows of product information and manufacturing materials	Presale customer communications, order processing, forecasting procedures, inventory and scheduling policies, shop floor layout, shipping and billing paperwork
Support	Deployment of expertise and availability of supplies and materials	Inventory of sales aids customers use; design of pull-through marketing programs Records of customer product-use experience, product-use knowledge, diagnostic tools, regulatory expertise
Pricing	Policies and cost structure	Pricing structure and terms, sales incentive programs, accuracy of price estimates, margin guidelines, actual cost levels and drivers, overhead allocation methods

then, by a process of elimination based on the collection of data on each, figuring out which causes apply and which have the greatest impact. This risks having to repeat the process should a possible cause not be defined at the outset. Failure to identify a key cause is especially likely when it's perceived as sensitive or off-limits.

Conjecture about possible causes can be intellectually appealing, and staying within the realm of supposition is safe. But the quickest way to get at the origins of a performance gap starts with what happens on the shop floor, the shipping dock, the lab bench, and at the receiving end of customers' telephone calls.

Pinpointing the Origins of Customer Value Gaps

Product or service attributes as defined by customers indicate where to look and what to look for. Discussion and review of actual experience, possibly supported by real-world testing, point to the source of gaps between attributes sought and those delivered. Real-world tests include actually using a product, placing a telephone call as if a customer, and tracking a real order.

Such analysis can reveal factors that no one knew affected delivery of customer value. For example, suppose customers seek order acknowledgment within a week, but the team finds that it takes as much as three weeks to dispatch that acknowledgment. Someone in customer service might attribute it to the computer being slow, and a data-processing person might explain that it's not the computer, since orders can be acknowledged overnight. All that remains between order entry and dispatch of the acknowledgment is the sales managers' review of the orders entered each day. When sales managers are on the road, the lists pile up on their desks, waiting for them to get to the office. They didn't know that their absence affected customers' views of company performance.

Repeated probing—asking *why?* several times—may be unnecessary to uncover the origin of a performance gap. Customers of a midsize manufacturing company faulted it for delivering later than the dates quoted. An examination of records for a sample of orders processed during the previous year uncovered the underlying reason for this:

▲ The lead time quoted was always an understatement. It covered only the time it took to manufacture and test the product, excluding the time needed to transmit orders internally, prepare the shipment, and transport it. This suggested that the remedy was to work on reducing the time to manufacture and test the product or to ask customers to place orders sooner based on the full current lead time. Requiring customers to make changes to suit the company, rather than the other way around, sounded like a quick and easy solution. However, this would not only represent the opposite of customer orientation but implied the company's current lead time was right, which further probing showed not to be the case.

▲ As much as 50 percent of the lead time—from customers placing an order until they received shipment—was to obtain materials. This suggested that the remedy was to work with vendors to shorten their lead times, except that these vendors provided materials for other products and consistently delivered them promptly.

▲ The real reason for the gap was finally revealed: a management policy banning purchase of manufacturing materials before receipt of a customer order. Changing that policy would reduce the full lead time by as much as ten weeks, making it possible to quote a shorter lead time that the company would be able to live up to.

Pinpointing the origin of gaps may require detailed operational analysis. For example, the underlying reason for a shortfall in product quality—which shows up as shoddy workmanship—might actually be caused by lack of training, poor production line layout, equipment that doesn't hold its setting, or the complexity of product design.

Analysis of a more technical nature reveals whether making additional products wanted by customers is within the capability of existing equipment and, if not, why this is so. A company whose customers sought the benefits of one-stop shopping found that a particular piece of equipment could not handle parts over a certain size.

Technical analysis also indicates whether current products can be revised to incorporate features that customers seek and, if not, why not. A company whose customers sought products in unbreakable containers, which no supplier provided, knew that a suitable material already existed, but found that it had not been tested fully.

Analysis of existing financial data uncovers the components of the company's cost structure that determine the profitability of sales in a particular customer segment. At a company supplying a product with its own brand name as well as a private-label version, the private-label product's lower gross margins made it appear less profitable. Yet customers purchasing private-label products serve end users that this company wouldn't reach through other channels and that represent a growing portion of total demand. The difference between manufacturing this company's own brand product and manufacturing the private-label version is minimal: the purchase cost of certain packaging materials, which are printed differently for each private-label customer. However, the purchase cost differential is far less than the costs associated with selling, marketing, processing orders for, and shipping the brand-name product. Unlike customers that purchase brand-name products, private-label customers place few orders for large quantities on a regular schedule, pay shipping costs, and do their own advertising and promotion. Therefore, when seen in terms of the bottom line and customer segments, private-label products are a significant profit generator for this company, not just a minor contributor to coverage of overheads as had been believed. Cost allocation methods had presented a misleading picture of where to focus, either on lowering net price to customers while maintaining margins or on increasing operating margins while holding prices steady.

Additional research and analysis reveal what drives the consumption of resources accounted for as overhead. These drivers (e.g., product revision frequency, order size, customer contacts per order, the number of materials suppliers) indicate where cost-reduction efforts would be most fruitful. Yet these must be approached with care. Overhead cost reductions can backfire in the same way that reducing so-called variable costs can, such as when elimination of an ingredient detracts from how the product performs for customers. A broad swath with a meat cleaver eliminates fat, but when it affects delivery of value to customers, it's the equivalent of cutting into the organization's muscle, nerves, and bone. For example, an electronics manufacturer making across-the-board head-count cuts avoided this danger by deciding to make an exception, exempting the equipment maintenance department from cutbacks. Cuts in this department would have detracted from the company's ability to provide the product delivery performance that key customers sought.

Acknowledging Reasons for Performance Gaps

The reasons for a customer value gap vary from company to company and defy speculation. Some key reasons are likely to be sensitive, but knowing what they are means knowing what the company's performance hinges on. The origins of value gaps fall into categories, as shown below:

Management mechanisms	Policies, procedures, and paperwork; measurements and their use; information and control systems; meetings and other day-to-day communications
Organization	Roles and responsibilities; rewards and recognition; reporting relationships; standards of behavior
People	Knowledge, skills, experience, interests, work styles (soloist or team player, self-starter or follow-the-leader)
Physical facilities	Office and plant layout and locations; machinery and equipment, computers
Procurement	Purchased supplies, materials, and sourcing

Value gap origins that fall in the first two categories are so common as to seem endemic to organizations. All companies suffer to some degree from cumbersome policies and procedures and inadequate communications, but dysfunctional role definitions, counterproductive performance measurements, an inappropriate reward system, and unclear or unassigned responsibilities are just as common—and more problematic. Such problems often remain unresolved until their pivotal effect on serving customers is recognized.

Historical emphasis on resource efficiency has left a harmful and pervasive legacy. Performance measurements and functional roles established years ago for internal control purposes can foster provincialism that restrains the organization's performance for customers or even encourages parochial action that conflicts with customers' priorities. For example:

▲ When marketing managers perceive their primary responsibility to be developing creative sales promotions, they're likely to ignore the practical impact of these programs, such as the administrative burden on customers and how cutoff dates affect production planning activities and cause peaks in capacity requirements.
▲ Emphasis on low indirect labor and high machine utilization in manufacturing discourages work on product and process developments needed to serve customers and encourages the production of large batches, which actually impedes material flow for timely delivery and raises inventory levels.
▲ With a narrow definition of its role in terms of novelty and technology, R&D is likely to concentrate on coming up with a next-generation product instead of on developing product revisions that meet customers' needs and can be produced at appropriate cost levels.

People on the investigating teams already have insight into value gap origins that relate to management mechanisms and to organization, seeing their effects from day to day. The perspective from lower down differs from that higher up, meaning that what a team finds may be news to upper management. Hearing such reasons articulated can be discomforting: They may put the reasons for gaps squarely on management's plate. Addressing these reasons, especially the use of business performance measurements, can have as great an effect on the company's performance as changes related to more concrete factors such as plant, equipment, and materials. And though they are more troublesome for members of senior management, changes in organization and management mechanisms can be considerably cheaper.

At this stage, such changes are only food for thought. A final determination can be made only after an overall direction has been determined and priorities established accordingly. Only senior management can define adjustments to departmental roles and responsibilities, organizational structure, performance measurements, and the reward system. However, the investigating teams propose how to redefine operational measurements to reflect the customers' perspective and how to reallocate certain tasks.

Results of the research to trace the origins of a performance gap can be captured on a chart such as that in Figure 2-7.

Developing Tailor-Made Approaches to Accomplish Needed Changes

Having identified the origins of a gap between customer value sought and what the company currently provides, a team has defined *what* needs to change. Its next task is to propose *how*: the ways, or approaches, to accomplish needed changes.

People throughout the organization have probably been coming up with some excellent ideas all along, before this investigation started. However, these ideas may not have surfaced or, if they did, they may not have been adopted because their relevance to

Figure 2-7. Origins of a customer value gap.

Product or Service Attribute Sought	Origins of Gap
Easy removal of product from package in correct orientation (currently packed with Styrofoam peanuts)	Final packing instructions call for filler but don't stipulate orientation Purchasing department performance is evaluated on low cost per unit
Rapid alignment for initial placement with integral fasteners	Current product configuration isn't suited to customer use of locating fixture to position the product for assembly Current tooling limitation
Few installation points that are easily accessible with unique fit-up	No one on staff has experience in product design for ease of assembly

serving customers wasn't recognized. For example, someone may have proposed adopting a different pallet-stacking pattern to get trucks loaded faster and on the way to customers more quickly, but never received the go-ahead to put the suggestion into practice. In the course of identifying the origins of performance gaps, creative juices have started to flow, putting minds and imaginations to work—consciously or unconsciously—on the product or service attributes being investigated. This means that development of approaches to effect needed changes has already started.

Brainstorm sessions can produce additional ideas: Being plugged into the internal grapevine means that team members know who the original thinkers are. People with firsthand knowledge of day-to-day activities often come up with innovative, elegantly simple ideas. At one company, shop floor personnel suggested performing a certain operation by hand for limited quantities rather than waiting for changeover of complex equipment and then having to discard or rework the first units produced because equipment settings needed fine-tuning. Switching to the manual operation would increase flexibility and responsiveness to schedule changes while increasing yield and reducing scrap.

Proposed approaches may be highly sophisticated, incorporating aspects of modern management techniques and tapping the potential of information technology. One manufacturing manager proposed grouping the equipment needed for a certain set of products, unwittingly applying the concept of manufacturing cells. At another company, a supervisor suggested a cross-training program to remove a bottleneck in production—a concept from just-in-time manufacturing. At yet another company, a member of the sales force who is a computer expert suggested a way to make product availability information residing on the mainframe computer accessible over the network. Whether old or new, humdrum or sophisticated, the approaches put forward relate directly to providing product and service attributes that matter to customers.

Approaches put forward by an investigating team may call for management guidance, especially if the team is working on Pricing. For example, customers using a company's products as manufacturing materials may be forced by the pricing structure to order larger quantities than desired. This presents customers with a lose-lose choice: hold higher inventory or miss out on discounts.

Analysis of the reason for this situation—discount levels set without consideration of customer use patterns—points to several approaches, some of which are, from management's perspective, more or less desirable. These include resetting price break points and restating qualifications for discounts in terms of dollar volume per order, or per year, instead of unit quantities of specific products.

Touching base with a team also allows management to reassure team members that innovative approaches are welcome and will be taken seriously and to ensure that a team's thinking isn't limited by company traditions.

When there are several underlying reasons for a customer-value gap, multiple approaches are needed to close it. For example, failure to provide spare parts within the time frame customers want can be attributed to a number of current practices:

▲ Manufacture of spares being fitted into the schedule if and when there is time
▲ Parts inventory being rifled to complete products for original equipment sales
▲ Production of parts for older models being discontinued

Such practices are in turn attributable to a number of underlying reasons:

▲ A bias in favor of original equipment manufacture
▲ Unassigned responsibility for forecasting and tracking demand for parts sold separately
▲ Sales force rewards that reflect sales of new equipment only
▲ Manufacturing equipment reconfigured for current models

How to address sales force priorities and rewards is for senior management to decide. Approaches to address some of the other reasons are self-evident, such as assigning responsibility for parts forecasting and tracking and revising production scheduling procedures. However, reinstituting production of parts for old models involves alternative approaches: It might be done in-house or by engaging subcontractors. Both these make-versus-buy options have merits and disadvantages. On the one hand, in-house manufacture is desirable, especially when demand for original equipment is low, but it requires reconfiguring equipment to accommodate parts for both old and current models. On the other hand, a good subcontractor that is accustomed to work of this kind might gear up quickly, but working with a new outside source requires close coordination.

Other types of a make-versus-buy choice might include the following:

▲ Establishing a service operation close to end-user locations or subcontracting after-sales service to an independent provider
▲ Developing a new product from scratch or licensing the technology
▲ Providing training for a current employee or hiring someone who already has the requisite skills

Keeping alternative approaches on the list means that the information needed to decide among them will be developed. The approaches proposed to accomplish needed changes can be added to the chart showing the results of value gap analysis, as shown in Figure 2-8.

▲   ▲   ▲

Once a team has defined the approaches to close a gap between customer value sought and provided, it next identifies what's involved in putting these approaches into practice.

Part C: Practical Matters—
Actions, Timing, and Resources

An investigating team determines the actions, timing, and resources involved in closing a gap between what customers seek and what the company can currently provide. This determination starts with identifying all aspects of implementation to define actions called for in any part of the organization. The teams then gauge overall timing and resource requirements. Part C is highlighted in Figure 2-9.

Figure 2-8. Approaches to close a customer value gap.

Product or Service Attribute Sought	Origins of Gap	Approach to Close Gap
Easy removal of product from package in correct orientation	Final packing instructions call for filler but don't stipulate orientation	Change packaging instructions Use new container that protects product without filler
	Purchasing department performance is evaluated on low cost per unit	Revise purchasing performance measurements to reflect low total cost
Rapid alignment for initial placement with integral fasteners	Current product configuration isn't suited to customer use of locating fixture to position the product for assembly	Reconfigure product
	Current tooling limitation	Acquire new tooling or Modify current tooling
Few installation points that are easily accessible with unique fit-up	No one on staff has experience in product design for ease of assembly	Subcontract product redesign

▲   ▲   ▲

Projecting resource requirements accurately without clearly defined actions on which to base them is tough. The result is rough approximations or projections that lack credibility for other reasons. When in doubt, the tendency is to overstate requirements. Requests for projected resource needs are often assumed to refer to *additional* resources. And when estimates are developed by each department separately, the sum can overstate the aggregate requirement. In contrast, estimates developed after a management decision has been made may be understated to tie in with what management is thought to want. In either case, key questions about estimates for resource requirements may be unposed or unanswered.

With the CORe Method, resource requirements are based on specific actions that are needed throughout the organization. This approach produces one set of estimates that is accurate and

Figure 2-9. Step Two—Concreteness: Scoping Out Needed Changes, Part C.

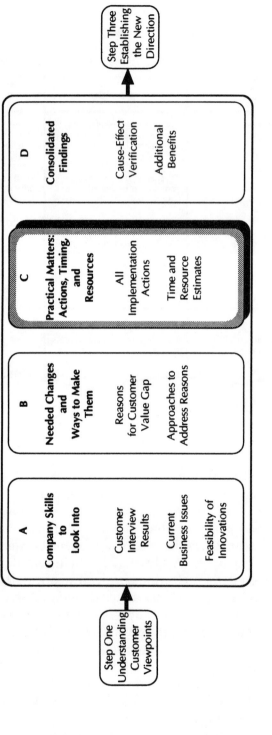

credible. These estimates cover only—but all—the resources involved in accomplishing changes to provide greater value for customers.

Ensuring Full Definition of Implementation

Identifying all facets of implementation reveals actions that, if overlooked, will ultimately cause results to fall short of expectations. Omission of any facet at this stage can lead to surprises, delays, and cost overruns when implementation is under way. For example, a company setting up an offshore production operation to serve remote customers concentrated on the financial, human resources, and engineering aspects of the project. When the project was almost complete, the company found that there were few suitable sources of materials nearby. This meant that either materials would have to be transported from another location or plant start-up would be delayed until relationships with suitable local vendors could be established.

Involving all functions in defining the extent of implementation ensures that all applicable aspects are identified and that timing and resource estimates are as accurate as possible. It also minimizes the likelihood that unplanned work on implementation will drain resources away from timely and cost-effective provision of current products and services.

Taking Advantage of In-House Expertise

Having the cross-functional teams identify time and resource requirements produces sound estimates as quickly as possible. People at lower levels—the people who will work directly on implementation—already have or can get the necessary information. For example, in an industry where manufacturing process revisions are subject to regulation, the approval process can determine when a change goes into effect. The people who work on such revisions may already know what test data have to be developed, how they are to be documented, and what's involved in shepherding a change through to final approval.

Even when a change is of a type not made before, these people know where to start finding out what's required. Knowing who to go to and what to ask for makes it possible to communicate effectively with outside entities (material suppliers, equipment manufacturers, regulatory bodies), and to develop solid estimates with them. The people in the best position to gauge the time and resources required are therefore those who'll play a part in implementation. This might include members of the management team. Should resource additions be called for to enable the company to provide greater value for customers, the time to find and hire someone with the requisite expertise could be a significant part of overall timing.

Meticulous precision is unnecessary: informed judgment and firsthand knowledge of what's involved in full implementation provide the basis for time and resource estimates that are inherently more accurate than precise figures for only a few aspects of implementation.

Involving people from various functions and at several levels in defining the extent of implementation has other important effects. First, having the teams identify what it will take to accomplish needed changes provides insight into who the key players might be. These people may be found in unexpected places:

▲ Someone in marketing might have particular aptitude for and interest in helping people use computers.
▲ Somebody in purchasing with a strong service orientation— who currently keeps track of vendor order completions— might be a candidate for a role in the administrative side of technical support.
▲ Someone's leadership ability—and the acceptance of it by others—might become apparent. Thus, you might find that a person in finance or sales would be an excellent candidate to play a leading role in product development efforts.

The second positive side effect of broad participation has to do with minimizing resistance to change. Although a certain department might play only a minor role in implementation, recognizing that its activities will be affected helps guard against NIH (not-invented-here) reactions. For example, when adopting a new production planning system to improve delivery performance, manufacturing, distribution, and data processing will play key roles in implementation. But conferring with marketing and finance (which use data from the system) shows them that their views are being considered. Giving people a voice in planning doesn't guarantee their commitment, but it does reduce the likelihood that the perception of being excluded will be a stumbling block in implementation.

Having the people who'll be involved in or affected by implementation develop the time and resource estimates has a third side benefit: greater effort to adhere to the estimates. Most people are likely to try harder to keep within time or cost figures if they had a say in developing them. Those numbers carry their personal stamp, which makes keeping to them a matter of professional pride.

Defining a Unique Set of Actions

Just as the approaches to accomplish customer-oriented changes are tailor-made for the company, so are the actions involved in implementation and, consequently, the time it will take. Each company has a different starting point. At one company, for example, engineers had already come up with designs for an all-new product concept, which meant that this early and time-consuming task was not required.

When defining what's involved in effecting key changes, seemingly mundane actions (e.g., modifying information flows, revising written reports) should get just as much attention as topics perceived to be glamorous (e.g., new equipment, new products, advanced technology). The aim is to enhance the company's ability to serve customers rather than simply add to its assets and resources. Only execution of all needed actions will enhance the company's performance for customers and financially.

Actions related to the use of new equipment (e.g., vendor selection, installation, testing, training) tend to come to mind as a matter of course simply because they are likely to involve a considerable amount of time and a sizable resource commitment. But implementation actions that are usually considered commonplace must also be identified. These might include:

▲ Redefining equipment set-up procedures
▲ Updating product information sheets

▲ Revising authorized signature levels for issue of low-value purchase orders or for dispatch of product samples to new customers
▲ Altering the paperwork used to record customer complaints or to transmit orders internally

Identifying all such actions, even when the time or resources involved are minor, makes it possible to gauge overall requirements fully and, once decisions on direction are made, develop an action plan that is comprehensive, cohesive, and detailed enough to guide implementation.

Additional activities that apply after changes have been accomplished must also be considered. For example, when new equipment or more sophisticated software is installed and in use, keeping it up and running implies a continuing work load (more elaborate equipment maintenance, centralized database administration). Once a new supplier is signed up, the need to work with that supplier remains. And when a new operational measurement that embodies the customer viewpoint has been designed, the tasks of compiling, documenting, and using that measurement are ongoing. Identifying such postimplementation activities ensures definition of the work load associated with not only closing the gap between customer value sought and delivered, but also keeping it closed. This provides a full foundation for estimation of resource requirements.

Gauging Comprehensive Resource Estimates

Order-of-magnitude resource estimates based on implementation actions throughout the organization and associated continuing activities provide more accurate information for decision-making purposes than piecemeal projections that are accurate to the nth degree. Accuracy to the last dollar or square foot is not worth waiting for when reliable estimates can be generated in a fraction of the time.

There are three resource types: people's time, equipment and space, and money (investment and working capital and out-of-pocket expenses). Except for money, resource requirements can be defined in units other than dollars. Conversion into dollars (from square feet or man-days) requires knowledge of figures that are usually closely guarded, if not strictly confidential. However, estimates of the dollar amounts associated with, for example, purchase of a certain piece of equipment or the probable cost of a product obtained from a subcontractor are readily obtainable and don't require elaborate calculations. Approximations of the promotional funding to launch a new product can be generated through a combination of inside experience and discussion with the company's advertising agency. A team can also estimate, perhaps with some number-crunching help, the financial exposure that comes with revising a purchasing policy to have materials on hand in anticipation of customer orders or the approximate value of a finished goods inventory increase before introduction of a product revision.

How much equipment time to allow to make manufacturing process refinements or conduct pilot manufacture for a new product can be based on prior experience. Space requirements to store products or spare parts and house personnel close to customer locations, for example, can also be arrived at using current knowledge or local norms and estimations of likely product quantities.

Development of resource estimates for alternative approaches will allow you to weigh their merits and disadvantages. For example, such estimates would show the out-of-pocket costs and approximate number of people involved in reconfiguring or upgrading existing equipment versus buying new, or the cash-time trade-offs that pertain during implementation of a more sophisticated production planning system. Doing training and forms design work in-house would incur a lower cash cost, but using outside help would be faster. Resource estimates for actions related to each approach can be captured on a chart such as that shown in Figure 2-10.

A team may also have suggestions about reducing the demand on existing resources. For example, the sales and marketing activities needed to establish relationships with customers in a new distribution channel would take an intense short-term effort and involve a continuing responsibility. However, relying more heavily on the company's advertising agency would allow insiders

Figure 2-10. Estimates of time and resource requirements to close a customer value gap.

Approach to Close Gap	Implementation Actions	Estimated Time	Estimated Resources
Change packaging instructions	Draft, test, finalize instructions		Write-off of current container inventory $ _____ (if not returned for credit or sold)
Use new container that protects product without filler	Obtain, test, and approve samples of new container Order and receive commercial quantities	5–7 weeks	Packing materials cost increase of $ _____ per unit
Revise purchasing measurements to reflect low total cost	Develop new measurements, review, approve, and explain		
Reconfigure product for customer use of locating fixture to position the product for assembly	Define reconfiguration, create new drawings, conduct tolerance study Run manufacturing pilot, perform functional test, release drawings and new parts list, update inspection procedures Monitor initial production closely and make refinements as needed Update and replace maintenance manuals and provide conversion kits for field service	6–7 months	Design/manufacturing engineers (both full time for 6–7 months); quality assurance and purchasing engineers (25% time for 6–7 months);accounting person (minimal); multiple production people (sporadic); technical writer (minimal)
Acquire new tooling or Modify current tooling	Design, purchase, test new tooling or Determine how to modify tool to retain multifunctionality, modify, and test Build inventory to cover demand while tool is unavailable		$10,000 (cash) Toolroom—one person (50% for 1 month) Inventory write-off old configuration ≤ $ _____

to focus on work that can be done only by company personnel. And providing the technical support customers seek calls for people proficient in problem-solving. These people may not currently have customer contact—they typically work in such functions as engineering, manufacturing, and quality assurance—but the people working on or with a team probably know of individuals who have the necessary knowledge and skills.

Estimates developed by the teams are only for resources associated with accomplishing needed changes. Whether resource additions to increase capacity are needed and warranted for the longer term will be part of management deliberations when deciding on direction and how best to allocate existing resources in light of overall priorities. Thus, any resource addition identified here is for a capability that is lacking and crucial to providing the product and service attributes being investigated. Such capabilities might include knowledge of the application of a particular product or process technology, skill in developing pull-through marketing programs for certain end users, or equipment capable of handling certain materials, performing certain manufacturing operations, or conducting repair service tests.

▲   ▲   ▲

Having identified the full extent of implementation and the actions it calls for and gauged the time and resources these actions involve, each team assembles the results of its work.

Part D: Consolidated Findings

The investigating teams summarize the information on needed changes. Each team accumulates its findings and verifies that these are complete and accurate. The findings of the teams are then reviewed together to identify any overlap. Part D is highlighted in Figure 2-11.

▲   ▲   ▲

Validating Conclusions

Use of the CORe Method results in a considerable amount of information on a customer value element. But the logical way in which this information was developed makes compiling a summary relatively straightforward. The compilation lays out the key conclusions and the rationales behind them in an orderly format such as that shown in Figure 2-12.

Reviewing the summary with the people who helped develop the information confirms that it is valid and complete. Revisiting the connections between cause and effect verifies that the approaches to accomplish needed changes are proper. Thinking through all aspects of implementation confirms that the actions needed throughout the organization have been defined and that time and resource estimates are comprehensive.

Figure 2-11. Step Two—Concreteness: Scoping Out Needed Changes, Part D.

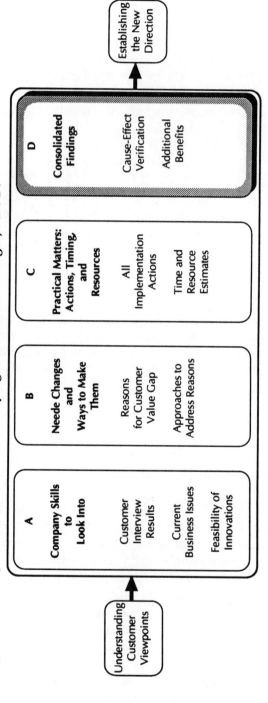

Figure 2-12. Summary of customer value gap analysis.

The company performs metal-working operations for prime contractors supplying the government. The primes work with subcontractors that perform a limited number of operations on specific parts. The primes are aiming to reduce costs through, for example, lower inventory levels, streamlined purchasing, and simplified internal coordination. Subcontractors are participating in these efforts. Assisting the primes' efforts by becoming an integrated supplier of certain parts would be an innovation for the company and make it the first in its supplier category to do so.

Product or Service Attribute Sought	Origins of Gap	Approaches to Close Gap	Actions	Estimated Time	Estimated Resources
Dramatically faster turnaround time* Fewer suppliers	Inability to perform upstream operations	Develop upstream capability in-house	Specify, obtain, install equipment		Senior management time (moderate throughout) plus production, quality assurance engineering (extensive), purchasing and sales (moderate)
			Identify, hire, orient key people		10,000 sq. ft. ($20 per sq. ft. rental if additional)
			Create, test, validate all manufacturing instructions, quality assurance procedures	>1 year <2 years	$1.5 million capital for equipment (plus $500,000 for land/ building purchase if additional)
			Obtain regulatory and customer approvals		$100,000 a year new hires (mfg. manager, engineer); includes fringes
					$50,000 out of pocket (search firm fees, travel, relocation costs)
		Make an acquisition	Screen/short-list acquisition candidates		Senior management and accounting time (extensive for 12 months, then moderate) plus production control and quality assurance (extensive) and purchasing and engineering (moderate) during and after integration plus sales (moderate)
			Make selection and conduct negotiations		
			Arrange financing, do due diligence, complete acquisition	18 months– 2 years	$3-4 million capital for acquisition
			Integrate operations, including government reporting and customer interactions†		$200,000 out of pocket (legal and accounting fees, investment banker, travel)
		Arrange joint venture/alliance	Screen, approach, negotiate with partner/ ally		Senior management and accounting time (extensive for 3-6 months, then moderate) plus production control, quality assurance, purchasing, and engineering (extensive for 6-12 months, then tapering)
			Establish operational procedures and responsibilities and integrate systems	6-12 months	$100,000 out of pocket (legal fees, travel)

*This would allow customers to hold significantly lower safety-stock inventory (a single part can be worth tens of thousands of dollars).
†Organizational integration to proceed in parallel with operational integration (and be completed after it).

The fact that the focal point of the investigation was product or service attributes of value to customers means that the effects of the proposed changes are primarily of benefit to customers. These effects, therefore, are also stated in customers' terms (e.g., longer product life, speedier in-use problem solving, volume discounts tied in with desired order patterns). However, a second look at a team's findings can reveal that a change designed to provide greater value to customers also offers benefits of internal significance. For example, when investigating the Transaction, the team might have proposed a new maintenance program for a particular piece of manufacturing equipment to prevent interruptions and production delays and thus enable the company to provide better delivery performance. This new maintenance program will also raise manufacturing yields, reduce costs of rework or scrap, and allow lower safety-stock inventory. Identification of such internal benefits makes the new maintenance program more cost-effective than it first appeared.

Since each investigating team concentrated on a specific customer value element and its associated company capability, having the teams review their findings together can reveal commonality among them. Overlap among the changes needed for different value elements can suggest ways to streamline implementation. For example, the team working on Pricing might have identified a key driver of costs related to serving a particular customer segment to be the number of contacts needed to assist customers with product installation. Ways to reduce the number of contacts might include rewriting set-up instructions and making certain product revisions to facilitate assembly, such as clear markings to identify each part.

These cost reduction changes are mostly in the company's interests. Making product revisions to serve the company's purposes at the same time as revisions for customers (lighter weight, safety features) would minimize the number of revisions; simplifying and speeding implementation considerably.

Closing the Investigation on the Right Note

Validating the findings with the people who worked on and with the investigating teams serves several purposes. It's an opportunity to provide reassurance that projected resource requirements are understood to be only estimates. In addition, explaining that management selection among the proposed approaches will follow, and that the resulting decisions will be communicated, indicates that everyone's efforts are appreciated and that their suggestions and insights will be taken seriously.

Discussions in the course of verifying the conclusions can reveal skepticism or even pockets of potential resistance. Innovation of any kind often elicits negative reactions simply because it implies an element of risk. Approaches that differ from those used in the past are especially likely to be viewed with distrust. The very concept of putting customer value in—rather than squeezing cost out—can be a radical departure from what people are accustomed to. Thus, to some people, a necessary and viable change can be counterintuitive. Not all such qualms can be dispelled, but acknowledging and responding to them at this stage helps prevent natural resistance to change from impeding successful implementation.

▲   ▲   ▲

Once the teams have summarized and verified their findings, the last part of Step Two is complete. Together, the conclusions of Step One—The Context: Understanding Customer Viewpoints, and Step Two—Concreteness: Scoping Out Needed Changes, provide a complete foundation on which to set direction and make preparations to pursue it successfully. Charting this direction and preparing for implementation are described in Step Three—The Crux: Establishing The New Direction.

Recap of Step Two—Concreteness

In Step Two—Concreteness, you determined what it would take to accomplish the key changes needed for your company to provide value as defined by customers. Involving people at lower levels ensured that these changes were relevant and workable and that

Figure 2-13. Step Two—Concreteness: Scoping Out Needed Changes, recap.

Part	What You Achieved and How
A Company Skills to Look Into	Defined the focus of the internal analysis and the number of investigating teams by: ▲ Identifying the product and service attributes that matter most to customers, especially an attribute for which customer needs are unmet or the company's performance falls short ▲ Considering current business issues and the feasibility of innovations
B Needed Changes and Ways to Make Them	Determined how to accomplish the changes needed to provide specific product or service attributes by: ▲ Tracing the origins of the gap between what customers seek and what the company can currently provide ▲ Developing approaches to address these reasons, including alternative approaches where applicable
C Practical Matters: Actions, Timing, and Resources	Defined the actions, timing and resources needed to implement the approaches and close the customer value gap by: ▲ Identifying the actions required for full implementation ▲ Gauging the time and resources these actions involve, including candidates for key roles in implementation, any cash-time trade-offs, and capabilities lacking and needed
D Consolidated Findings	Validated and summarized the conclusions and closed the internal analysis on a positive note by: ▲ Reviewing the findings with the people who worked on them to verify that the conclusions are complete and accurate ▲ Identifying internal benefits and overlap among the teams' findings to simplify and speed implementation ▲ Reconfirming that the views of people who'll be involved in or affected by the changes are being considered and that the estimates are for decision making only, the results of which will be communicated

the actions they required were stated in sufficient detail to develop a plan of action for implementation. This involvement also spread awareness of customers and of the need for change, fostering a sense of urgency, ownership, and participation among the people whose efforts will make implementation a success. Figure 2-13 summarizes what was done in Step Two.

Step Three

The Crux: Establishing the New Direction

The conclusions of Step One—The Context: Understanding Customer Viewpoints, and Step Two—Concreteness: Scoping Out Needed Changes, together feed Step Three. In Step Three, the pivotal step of the CORe Method, you switch from developing information to using it to make decisions, thereby starting the transition to action that will result in higher profits. It's here that you mesh planned action with the rest of the business before initiating implementation. Proper integration ensures that efforts to provide greater value for customers aren't a separate, additional program but a built-in part of how you run the business and how the company operates.

This step also builds confidence and accord among management team members and encourages their commitment to lead and support unified action to translate plans into progress and higher profits.

▲　　▲　　▲

Step Three has five parts:

Part A Which Customers? How to Attract and Keep Them?
Part B Blueprint for Action
Part C Resources for Customers, Profits for the Company
Part D Setting the Stage
Part E Management Team Sanction

An overview of the contents of this step is shown in Figure 3-1.
Working through Step Three produces decisions on how to serve current customers more effectively and profitably, which

Figure 3-1. Step Three—The Crux: Establishing the New Direction.

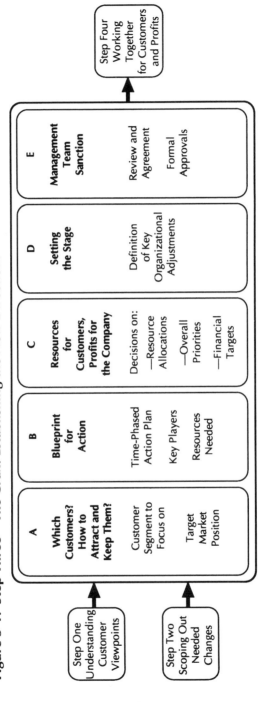

A	B	C	D	E
Which Customers? How to Attract and Keep Them?	**Blueprint for Action**	**Resources for Customers, Profits for the Company**	**Setting the Stage**	**Management Team Sanction**
Customer Segment to Focus on	Time-Phased Action Plan	Decisions on:	Definition of Key Organizational Adjustments	Review and Agreement
Target Market Position	Key Players	—Resource Allocations		Formal Approvals
	Resources Needed	—Overall Priorities		
		—Financial Targets		

Step One Understanding Customer Viewpoints

Step Two Scoping Out Needed Changes

Step Four Working Together for Customers and Profits

market areas to focus on, how to deploy resources more productively, what improvement in financial results can realistically be expected, and which organizational changes are most
crucial. Examples of specific questions that you answer in Step
Three are:

▲ Which new products or product revisions should we work
  on first?
▲ In the ____ market, we're on a par with two entrenched
  competitors and another is gaining share. What specifically
  do we need to do to strengthen—or at least maintain—our
  position?
▲ Where should we target marketing expenditures for the
  greatest bottom-line impact?
▲ Would it make sense to bring product development activities within the business unit, leaving basic research in R&D?
▲ Where in the market should we concentrate our resources
  for the greatest impact on the bottom line?
▲ How does this . . . (cost reduction, improvement program,
  investment) tie in with what matters to customers?
▲ Do we currently measure business performance in ways
  that *discourage* action focused on customers and bottom-
  line results?
▲ Where are the resource constraints going to be when
  we . . . (add this new product, enter a new market, increase
  sales with current customers)? Can we reallocate existing
  resources rather than add to them? What reallocations
  would remove the constraints without ill effect on customers—or on matters of internal concern?
▲ Are the priorities we have in effect now consistent with the
  company's goals? If not, how should these priorities be
  revised?
▲ Are the product development and improvement efforts we
  currently have under way really the most productive way
  for people to spend their time? How might they spend their
  time and energy more productively?
▲ Considering product launch costs in various markets, which
  should we focus on for the greatest impact on profits and
  returns?

▲ How might we reshape the organization to strengthen our standing with customers and enable us to compete more effectively?
▲ The proposed . . . (strategic alliance, acquisition, joint venture) is being talked about as a great opportunity for us. Is it? What would it enable us to do that we currently can't and that is worth the time and money?

The Key to Successful Implementation: Full Preparation

It's what happens *after* a course of action is defined that makes the difference between its success and failure. Actually realizing improved results depends on how well that course of action is implemented. This is where the best of intentions commonly go astray.

Ensuring that all the pieces are in place for smooth and effective implementation is a complex matter. What specifically is to be done, when, and by whom must be defined. In addition, action requires resources, and real-world limitations on resources raise questions about overall priorities. Changes to provide greater value for customers will be competing for resources with ongoing profit-generating activities and other improvement projects—as well as any efforts of significance to the company internally, such as adhering to governmental regulations on human safety and environmental matters. Only after resource allocations have been defined accordingly can the net financial impact be projected accurately and realistic targets determined. Unrealistic targets discourage commitment to achieve them.

Moreover, when the organizational infrastructure embodies yesterday's priorities, achievement of targeted results is undermined at the outset. Inconsistency between the current organizational infrastructure and unified action focused on customers and bottom-line results sends people mixed signals. Since the messages sent by that infrastructure carry great weight—signifying what senior management deems most important—implementation gets short shrift and progress falters. For many companies, the consequences are all too familiar. Initial enthusiasm becomes disenchantment. Team spirit disintegrates into finger pointing. The consequent delays and cost overruns cause financial results to fall short of expectations, and management has nasty surprises to deal with.

But when priorities, resource allocations, and the organizational infrastructure are aligned with overall direction and the actions it calls for, people receive strong, clear, consistent signals. Implementation then gets the attention it needs to proceed expeditiously, and targeted improvements in performance and financial results actually materialize.

The First Preparation: Direction Decisions

Setting overall direction is the first preparation for action that produces bottom line benefits. Developing or overseeing the development of business strategy is a task that only senior line management can perform. No other position in the organization has the necessary combination of scope and influence, knowledge of the company's goals and resources, and orientation to the future and to bottom-line financial results.

Determining the direction a company or business unit is to take is hard work that calls for a mixture of creativity, intelligent use of facts, and tough-minded business judgment. Decisions that affect service to customers, the company's future, its employees' livelihood, and its suppliers' prospects can be daunting. Decisions must often be made based on partial or inconsistent information. It may be months before you can tell whether planned actions are working. And there's always an element of the unknown; to some extent, outcomes are always unpredictable.

As with any decision making, defining and establishing direction with the CORe Method are likely to involve iteration. By starting with a skeletal proposal to take a first look at the numbers you avoid spending time on a detailed proposal when order-of-magnitude calculations based on the best-case scenario (for volumes and pricing, for example) aren't good enough. "No-go" decisions are often easier to make—and are less risky. So if the rough-cut numbers look good, you then need to flesh out a full-blown proposal—perhaps with detailed, pro forma financial statements—on which to base a possible "go" decision. When developing the full-blown proposal, iteration may be needed to arrive at the best balance of feasibility and desirability.

Although decision making with the CORe Method is methodical, it's far from mechanistic. How many iterations and how much detail depend on what the numbers look like and your judgment. You could make a "no-go" decision as early as Part A of this step. But for a "go" decision, you'll need to complete all five parts.

Part A: Which Customers? How to Attract and Keep Them?

You define how best to position the company in terms of value for customers in an important segment or segments. Using the information developed in the preceding steps, you first ascertain whether a particular customer segment merits the level of attention and investment needed for your company to become or remain a leading supplier there. For such a segment, you then determine which customer value element to empha- size—the one that will give customers the greatest possible value, make the most of your company's current strengths, and achieve the best possible differentiation from competitors. Part A is highlighted in Figure 3-2.

▲ ▲ ▲

Some companies have only a vague sense of where they are going, others expend considerable time and effort developing and articulating their vision. But *how* a vision is to be realized is seldom spelled out in a sufficiently pragmatic way. Without down-to-earth strategies to accomplish it, the vision remains unreal. It lacks relevance to the very people whose actions determine whether it will be realized.

The position the company will target, defined in terms of customer value, spells out the organization's strategy for a partic- ular customer segment. This strategy is specific enough to have meaning to the people who will act on it and to develop an implementation plan. The strategy for a certain customer segment also furnishes managers at all levels with a frame of reference that provides direction for their day-to-day decisions.

Figure 3-2. Step Three—The Crux: Establishing the New Direction, Part A.

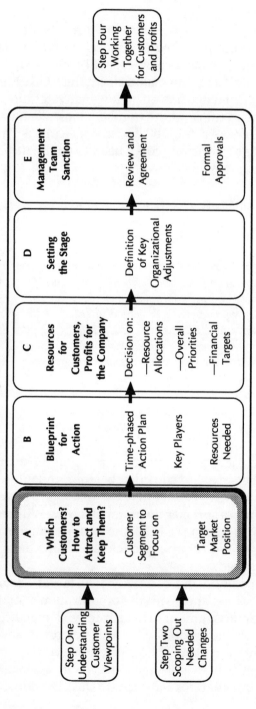

Step One
Understanding
Customer
Viewpoints

Step Two
Scoping Out
Needed
Changes

A

**Which
Customers?
How to
Attract and
Keep Them?**

Customer
Segment to
Focus on

Target
Market
Position

B

**Blueprint
for
Action**

Time-phased
Action Plan

Key Players

Resources
Needed

C

**Resources
for
Customers,
Profits for
the Company**

Decision on:
—Resource
Allocations

—Overall
Priorities

—Financial
Targets

D

**Setting
the Stage**

Definition
of Key
Organizational
Adjustments

E

**Management
Team
Sanction**

Review and
Agreement

Formal
Approvals

Step Four
Working
Together
for Customers
and Profits

Recognizing the Advantages of Customer-Oriented Strategies

Defining direction in terms of customers leaves no question that the primary objective is *customer* advantage. A customer-oriented strategy is therefore a business strategy aimed at delivering value to customers by building on the company's key capabilities as perceived by customers. A customer-oriented strategy is specific to a certain customer segment and encompasses narrow, functional-type initiatives such as a product development project, a manufacturing investment, a promotional campaign, or a program to improve after-sales service. In addition, a customer-oriented strategy is about serving real customers—the ones that produce revenue—rather than how parts of the organization serve one another.

Strategies that are defined in terms of the company commonly cause confusion and may or may not tie in with value for customers. Does the company's or business unit's marketing or distribution strategy refer to how it distributes or markets its products or to activities within the distribution or marketing departments? What are such "strategies" intended to do for which customers?

It is questionable whether inwardly focused strategies will move the company closer to its growth and profit goals. For example, a product launch strategy typically has an internal objective (introduce the product) and an end date (completion of the launch) that are probably irrelevant to customers.

Since the needs and priorities of customers in one segment invariably differ from those of customers in another, where and how a new product is introduced determines how successful it will be. To customers who are satisfied with products they currently use but are looking for faster and more consistent supply, the new product is less relevant than improved delivery. And to customers for whom the new product does offer advantages, the launch itself matters far less than how effectively the product meets their needs over time—as part of an overall value package.

It is essential therefore to see a product launch as just one component of the company's business strategy—that is, how it will provide value to customers in a certain segment. This underscores the fact that the new product itself is only one factor in customers' decision making, which also includes pre- and post-sale support, prompt availability of supplies or parts, and pricing consistent with the economic impact of switching to and using the new product.

Just as a customer-oriented strategy encompasses all elements of customer value, it also encompasses all parts of a business unit. Such a strategy, therefore, provides the foundation for developing a comprehensive implementation plan—one that contains actions needed throughout the organization. In the case of a new product, seeing the launch as part of a business strategy to serve customers effectively indicates how best to promote, package, supply, service, and revise the product. Clearly, this involves the efforts not only of sales and marketing and product development but also of materials management, field service, order processing, and manufacturing.

Several parts of the organization also have a role in other efforts to improve business performance, such as faster product delivery, product revisions, cost reductions, and entry into a new market area. A cohesive, customer-oriented action plan for all functions therefore provides the basis to allocate resources more productively and to project bottom-line financial benefits realistically. By refocusing existing resources to the greatest extent possible, you minimize the need for additions, thereby maximizing the potential increase in profitability and investment returns.

Having strategies defined in terms of customers also provides a framework to screen proposed improvement programs and investments to avoid those that are of minimal significance to customers and of marginal financial benefit. Even more important than avoiding questionable proposals is identifying the most beneficial initiatives: those that focus on the customer segments that are and will be most valuable to the company and on the product and service attributes that matter most.

Key Players in Strategy Development. Directing people and activities has to do with managing: To a manager, direction and the priorities that flow from it are a given. However, charting direction has to do with planning and is a crucial task that distinguishes leading from managing. Moreover, such planning—defining direction to see what the company or business unit needs to work on first—is one of the toughest parts of running a business and can only be done effectively by the management team. Defining direction in a group effort by the general manager with his or her direct reports can be a radical departure from customary practice. With the CORe Method, the functional heads are already familiar with the information on which strategies are based, which makes it easier for each person to participate. Participation means more than being in the room. The person taking the lead has to foster open discussion and encourage the reticent people to speak up. This implies listening objectively to the ideas and insights of other people, who may be reluctant to speak out against what they think the boss wants. Exercising a strong personality, a loud voice, and a higher rank defeats the purpose. At one such session with all the preparatory work complete, the president—anxious to have the matter done with and reach a conclusion—dominated with ill effect.

What started as a session to come up with two strategies—one for an attractive new market area and one to strengthen the company's position and profitability in the core business—resulted in no strategy being defined. Instead, the conclusions were a mandate to manufacturing to use cheaper materials and a mandate to sales to make more calls. The only functional head who felt he'd participated fully was the director of finance. Full participation of each functional head makes for better strategy—two heads are better than one—that balances optimism with realism and desirability with feasibility. Full participation also builds consensus and confidence and, with these, a broad sense of ownership.

Developing customer-oriented business strategies is neither mysterious nor magical. It doesn't involve esoteric theories or elaborate modeling. Figure 3-3 shows the key inputs and outputs when defining direction in terms of customers. The purpose in strategy development is (1) to confirm that a customer segment warrants a certain level of attention and investment and (2) to determine the emphasis to put on each customer value element so as to serve customers effectively and thereby match or beat key competitors.

Customer-oriented strategies may differ dramatically from those your company pursued in the past or those that worked for

Figure 3-3. Defining direction in terms of customers—inputs and outputs.

Inputs	Direction Questions	Outputs
Customer Segment Attractiveness The size, growth, degree of competition, and profit margins inherent in a customer segment *Customer Viewpoint* By segment, customers' • Key criteria for purchase decisions • Assessment of suppliers' performance • Objectives and unmet needs *Company Time and Resources* The time and resources required for the company to provide the key product and service attributes sought by customers in a particular segment *Competitor Situation* Key competitors' probable performance for customers in a particular segment and likely reactions to other suppliers' actions	*Customer Opportunities—Where?* Does a customer segment warrant the level of attention/investment needed for the company to become or remain a leading supplier? • Is a segment that warrants investment a primary or secondary candidate? • Should a segment that doesn't warrant investment receive its current level of attention or a lower level? *Customer Opportunities—What?* Which customer value element(s)–or product and service attributes–should the company emphasize or deemphasize in a particular customer segment?	*Customer Segment Importance* How important a customer segment is and will be to the company *Target Market Position* For an important segment, the position in customers' eyes the company will aim for in order to • Provide value for customers • Make the most of its strengths • Match or beat key competitors *Focus for Action Planning* The product or service attributes needing action to attain or maintain the company's target position in an important customer segment

Note: Inputs come from Steps One and Two of the CORe Method as follows:

Customer Segment Attractiveness—Step One, Parts A and B
Customer Viewpoint—Step One, Part C
Company Time and Resources—Step Two, Parts C and D
Competitor Situation—Step One, Part D

Other inputs are the resources available to the company, or obtainable, and the company's financial objectives.

other companies or with other customers. Keeping an open mind is therefore essential to avoid personal preference, emotion, and opinion clouding the thinking. The strategies that will work for your organization are based on hard facts and hard-headed—but not necessarily cold-hearted—judgment. They are about the future rather than the past, and they may break new ground rather than take the beaten track.

Assessing Customer Segment Importance

Early on in Step One—The Context: Understanding Customer Viewpoints, you screened out customer segments that offered poor profit potential for your company, specifying which were to be looked into in depth. The question here is: Does a certain customer segment warrant the level of attention and investment needed for your company to be a leading supplier? (The time and resources this would require were identified in Step Two.) This question applies to customer segments currently served as well as new ones.

Decisions to enter a customer segment entirely new to the company, or to leave one it currently serves, are rare. Yet before making any significant resource commitment, it makes sense to confirm that a segment is likely to generate at least adequate returns. Moreover, knowing that a customer segment offers *high* returns makes it possible to focus ongoing activities accordingly. The basic idea is to allocate 80 percent of resources toward serving the 20 percent of customers that produce 80 percent of profits—both in the short term and in the foreseeable future.

Having found an attractive customer segment, the temptation is to take advantage of what it offers. Many a company has ventured into high-growth markets not knowing, or ignoring, what was really needed for it to succeed. And too many companies that find themselves in low-growth or highly competitive market areas continue to commit resources to them. Turning away from opportunities and deemphasizing yesterday's treasured customers are tough decisions. But thoughtfully selecting which customer segments to invest in for the future—and which to deemphasize—

lets you build a strong position rather than commit resources to try to fix a weak one.

If your company currently serves one of the most attractive customer segments as a leading or second-tier supplier, you may need to make only incremental improvements involving limited time and resources to cement or strengthen your standing with customers. In this instance, there's little doubt that this customer segment is important. However, when remaining or becoming a leading supplier requires a major effort and investment, targeting a customer segment with attractive size, growth, and profit margins may be more conceptually desirable than realistically worthwhile. In general, entering a segment with characteristics that vary greatly from those of the segments currently served, or investing in one in which the company's current capabilities fit poorly, requires special scrutiny. Specifying a customer segment to deemphasize—one in which you'll continue merely to take orders or that you'll exit entirely—is as important as stipulating a segment that you *will* invest in.

Designating the customer segment or segments to do business in and to invest in is the equivalent of selecting your competitors. Clearly, the degree and nature of competition is a major factor in determining the chances for success in a certain segment. For example, knowing that a powerful new competitor is setting out to establish a beachhead, or that a formerly sleepy current competitor is now working directly on customers' priorities, suggests that a particular customer segment is probably less of an opportunity than it originally appeared. But when no other supplier appears to have identified an emerging customer segment as an opportunity—or when building the capabilities needed to strengthen your company's position in one segment would make it a strong contender in another—you might target a small segment that offers growth potential.

The larger the investment involved, the greater the need to specify the target customer segment or segments. It's essential to be sure that any major additional funding will strengthen your company's ability to deliver value for customers in a segment with inherent profit potential. This ensures that investments are made where the potential for generating returns is greatest.

Determining How to Attract and Keep Customers

The significance of decisions to enter, invest in, or leave a market area is obvious, but just as important—and more intellectually demanding—is specifying how to attract and keep customers within an important segment. You do this by determining which value element or elements your company will emphasize. This determination is based primarily on the fit between what matters most to customers and the company's strengths as perceived by them. Considering what it will take for the company to build on those strengths and thus provide superior value for customers ensures that the target position is realistic and financially worthwhile.

From the target market position flow the product and service attributes that need to be worked on first. These are the attributes whose improvement will have the greatest impact on the company's standing with customers; therefore, the resources committed to improvement efforts will be deployed most productively.

Developing a Target Market Position: Two Examples. EG Company manufactures computer peripherals. Its customers—middle managers in medium-size companies—are mostly unfamiliar with the use of personal computers and related equipment. (What follows has been simplified for purposes of illustration.)

Product and service attributes defined and ranked by EG Company's customers according to their significance in deciding among suppliers are:

1. *Product:* reliability and compatibility with products already on site supplied by other manufacturers
2. *Transaction:* prompt and accurate information on product availability and shipment on the date agreed to
3. *Pricing:* no-surprise prices (no periodic special offers, for example) and no-questions-asked warranty parts replacement
4. *Support:* access to technical support immediately after purchase (at no charge) and in-use problem solving (at customer expense)

The customers' current supplier ranking is illustrated in Figure 3-4.

The first consideration is that EG's target position should build on its current strength—in this instance, the Transaction, where EG Company ranks first. This would be the cornerstone of the target position in its first tentative version. The key to a higher standing with customers, however, is improved performance on their top-priority value element, the Product. The question is, how close would EG's improvement actions, as defined in Step Two, bring it to the ideal? In this case, attaining the ideal is *not* feasible in the short term, since achieving product compatibility would be a major undertaking. But making certain revisions could move EG's current product closer to the ideal of reliability (for example, by using longer-lasting materials to increase the longevity of key components).

Improved performance on Pricing (value element 3) and Support (value element 4) is also desirable but less crucial. Thus, the first pass at EG's target position would be second place on the Product, first place on the Transaction, second place on Pricing, and third place on Support.

The next consideration is the probable results of key competitors' improvement efforts. How well does EG's tentative target position stand up against the two principal competitors' probable *future* performance? More specifically, how likely is it that each of

Figure 3-4. Supplier performance assessment by EG's customers.

Customer-Ranked Value Elements	Customers' Supplier Ranking		
	1	2	3
1. Product	Co. A	Co. B	Co. EG
2. Transaction	Co. EG	Co. A	Co. B
3. Pricing	Co. B	Co. EG	Co. A
4. Support	Co. A	Co. B	Co. EG

these competitors will threaten EG Company's superiority in the Transaction and that Company A will strengthen its performance on Pricing? According to what was found out in Step One—The Context: Understanding Customer Viewpoints, Part D, Company A—an old-line supplier—is somewhat complacent, relying on its product superiority. Every indication is that it will continue on its current path. Company B, however, is another matter. It is more aggressive and savvy about customers' decision making and the growth potential that this segment offers. These customers are evidently important to Company B. Having achieved second position on the Product, B is now concentrating on delivery while continuing to improve its product to embody the customers' ideal. Overall, Company B is likely to surpass A in time but not to surpass EG's performance on the Transaction in the foreseeable future. Thus, EG's tentative position for this customer segment remains valid.

Figure 3-5 below shows EG Company's target market position, along with Company B's probable future standing. The arrow indicates where EG Company needs to strengthen its performance to realize this position and, therefore, the focal point for its improvement efforts.

The attributes a company needs to work on first provide the basis of its action plan, but it's vital to specify all the value elements

Figure 3-5. EG's target market position.

Customer-Ranked Value Elements	Target Position		
	1	2	3
1. Product	Co. A	Co. B/EG ◀━	
2. Transaction	Co. EG	Co. A/B	
3. Pricing	Co. B	Co. EG	Co. A
4. Support	Co. A	Co. B	Co. EG

in its target position. The cornerstone of target position—that is, a key value element where customers regard the company's performance to be strong—is what differentiates the company from its competitors in a positive and relevant way. Identifying the cornerstone ensures that adequate attention is given to maintaining a strength so that positive differentiation is sustained.

Overemphasis on improvement efforts for a value element where changes are needed is concentrating on weakness rather than strength. In the worst case, this could result in a competitor catching you off guard and usurping that edge. For EG Company, therefore, continuing to improve upfront customer communications and bringing on-time delivery even closer to 100 percent—while working to advance product reliability—would maintain its lead on the Transaction.

If product compatibility were feasible in a reasonable time, EG Company could realistically pursue a position consisting of leadership on the two top value elements. This suggests the possibility of pricing at a premium. But before jumping at that opportunity, the company would need to evaluate it in financial terms, that is, determine the probable impact on revenue and margins, against which the product development investment could be amortized. A comparison based on estimates obtained in Step Two—Concreteness: Scoping Out Needed Changes would be enough to tell whether incorporating the compatibility feature to realize twofold superiority would be financially desirable.

As a second example, consider XY Company, which makes components for transportation equipment. XY prides itself on the superior performance of its product, which includes energy efficiency, but this pride is only partially well-founded. In a market area that XY recently entered, customers identified fit and finish for ease of assembly as being as important as end-use product performance. Thus, the company's target market position would be based on product superiority even though improvement in fit and finish was needed there.

The other key area needing improvement to lift XY Company's standing with customers is delivery—their second most important consideration after the product itself. On the Transaction, the company's performance lags behind that of its top three competitors, meaning that strengthening that performance is crucial for the company to capitalize on the superiority of its product for end users. This superiority, generous marketing and technical support, and even low price would not be enough to retain customers who had to shut down their assembly lines due to late deliveries—or to attract new ones who'd heard of this happening. Thus, XY's target market position consists of maintaining its leadership on the Product, improving performance on the Transaction to match that of key competitors, and maintaining current performance on Support and Pricing.

The improvement action this position calls for implies some major changes in how the company operates. But, according to the conclusions of Step Two, changes to improve delivery performance could be accomplished with existing resources. With its roots in another market area, XY Company had traditionally designed products to order, which lengthens the time preceding the start of manufacture. In addition, past improvement efforts in manufacturing had aimed at reducing costs by maximizing resource utilization, meaning that large batch sizes now impede materials flow. An action plan based on the target position therefore includes:

▲ Standardizing product design of a limited number of models, in which the most commonly sought features are incorporated, and offering a shorter list of options so that products can be built to order from parts already in inventory

▲ Adopting new production planning parameters and taking other measures, such as reducing set-up time at bottleneck operations, to speed materials flow

▲ Providing training for the people who work at XY Company's own assembly operation—where any last-minute rush to make shipments could cause fit and finish problems—and authorizing them to set aside any problematic units

Improving product fit and finish and delivery performance would require an intense effort, but no additional resources.

Limited Options. When the scope for product differentiation is minimal, or when your company has little influence over the

characteristics of the products it handles, emphasizing a nonproduct value element is the only option. For example, a company that
distributes books to large institutions has to build on a service
strength. One such company already provides various Support-
type attributes that its competitors don't—posters appealing to
certain types of readers the institutions are trying to attract,
funding for prizes they award—but the institutions rank the
Transaction as more important. For them, prompt availability and
broad choice within the subjects of key interest to readers have
always been crucial considerations in selecting among distributors.
In addition, the objectives of many institutions now include
streamlining the procedure for ordering books.

Since the institutions value the Transaction more highly than
Support, this distributor's performance on the Transaction is its
most relevant strength in its market positioning. This strength is
based on, for example, the availability of books on tape and
videocassette—which offers the institutions a single source for all
formats—and prompt delivery from local warehouses. The distributors' expertise in using computers for inventory control can also
be turned to advantage for customers. Actions to build on its
Transaction strength would include providing the institutions
with computer terminals that are specially programmed and linked
with its own and training in their use. Being the first distributor to
do so would make it hard for competitors to catch up. Once
institutions are computer linked to a distributor providing broad
choice and prompt availability, they will have little need for a
second or third terminal linked to other distributors.

Competitors' Blind Spots. Validating a target market position
in light of competitors' likely capabilities might reveal that they are
strengthening their performance on the value element that you
initially selected as the cornerstone. This would challenge your
superiority, either invalidating the position entirely or causing it to
become outdated. To avoid this, you must either accentuate
another aspect of the cornerstone value element that's significant
to customers or select another value element as the basis of positive
differentiation.

Should a competitor have a technological or other capability
equal to or greater than your company's, selecting which value

element to emphasize takes particular care. You have to select one on which your performance is—or could be at acceptable cost—superior to competitors', where their capabilities don't apply or where, for some other reason, their performance is unlikely to improve dramatically.

For example, Company Z, which sells industrial chemicals to distributors, has two distinct types of competitors. The first type, the technology leaders, consistently introduce new products early, leapfrogging each other and racing to be the first with the latest. These established companies provide generous marketing and technical support and charge super-premium prices. The other type consists of small companies that sell certain nonproprietary products at rock-bottom prices and provide no support. Each type of competitor has an edge that Company Z cannot match: Company Z's introductions of new products lag behind those of the leaders, and its investments in product development and provision of marketing and technical support mean that its cost base is far higher than that of the low-price suppliers.

However, customers rank both types of competitors poorly on the Transaction. The distributors are working to reduce their operating costs and, therefore, rate highly those service attributes related to the Transaction. This, therefore, is the way for Company Z to provide value to customers and is the key to its positive differentiation. Making the Transaction the cornerstone of its position prompts distributors to turn first to Company Z and to use its competition only for individual leading-edge products or for specific commodity products for which there is particularly high end-user demand.

This company's achievement of Transaction superiority involves providing several attributes that neither type of competitor does or is likely to, including product line breadth, courtesy in dealings with customer personnel, flexible order quantities, and shipment of complete orders. Actions required to provide such attributes—and thus realize the requisite Transaction superiority—address the addition, for resale, of selected products from other manufacturers and the signing up of subcontract manufacturers to ensure continued product supply when peaks in demand exceed in-house capacity.

Clearly, emphasizing the Product, the Transaction, Support,

and nonprice aspects of Pricing is preferable to using absolute price levels as the differentiator, even when you are, or are aiming to be, a low-cost producer. Use of the in-depth knowledge of competitors' operations developed in Step One helps avoid having to differentiate on price.

The low-price competitors in the industrial chemicals company, for example, keep their costs down mainly by taking shortcuts in meeting regulatory requirements. Eventually their lack of regulatory compliance will catch up with them, causing interruptions in their product supply followed by cost and price increases. These competitors will then have an uphill climb trying to regain customers who have had to switch to other suppliers in the meantime. So by deciding against lowering its prices, Company Z—although losing some market share in the short term—continues to provide the marketing and technical support that these competitors don't, and its product quality is also more dependable. These factors, plus its outstanding performance on the Transaction, will do more to enhance Company Z's profits than short-term price cuts would. Moreover, continuing to provide nonprice attributes of value to customers also differentiates Company Z in a positive way: as a long-term player in the industry rather than a fly-by-night venturer out for a quick profit. As this company's situation shows, competitive considerations can confirm the target market position already defined rather than necessitate revising it.

Concluding Strategy Development

By defining and refining the position your company will aim for in a particular customer segment, you can arrive at the one that's best. That position will provide superior value for customers, build on the company's strengths in their eyes in ways that are doable and cost-effective, and provide positive and lasting differentiation from key competitors.

Written conclusions of this part of Step Three are useful right away to shape the plan of action to attain the target market position. And for future reference, a record is needed of the reasoning behind these conclusions—that is, behind the designation of an important customer segment and the definition of a target market position. But this record need not hold up development of the action plan. All that's needed for action planning is the target market position itself, such as that shown previously in Figure 3-5, annotated to show the specific product and service attributes that need improvement. These conclusions also provide the framework to evaluate proposed improvement efforts or resource commitments that await your review and approval.

In addition, now is the time to review any initiatives under preliminary discussion (a capital investment, product development project, new production planning approach) that are not yet concrete proposals, and to identify and call a halt to any embryonic project out of keeping with the new direction.

▲   ▲   ▲

Having designated an important customer segment and defined how to attract and keep those customers, you now have the company's business strategy for that segment. This strategy is a necessary, but not sufficient, preparation for action that will increase bottom-line results. Shaping the action plan to attain the target market position comes next.

Part B: Blueprint for Action

You map out a time-phased action plan to provide superior value for customers as called for in the target market position. Piecing together the pertinent actions defined in Step Two, you lay out the overall plan, showing actions and interactions needed throughout the organization. You then compress the timing where possible and identify minor tasks that would jeopardize effective implementation. The key player's roles are proposed and resource requirements aggregated according to when they're needed, with resource additions if applicable. Part B is highlighted in Figure 3-6.

▲   ▲   ▲

Without a comprehensive plan of action it's almost certain that implementation actions will founder. Needed changes won't be

Figure 3-6. Step Three—The Crux: Establishing the New Direction, Part B.

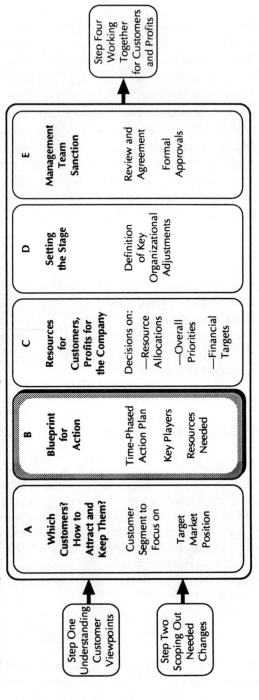

accomplished, performance improvement for customers will be minimal, and, consequently, potential profit gains won't materialize. The plan developed with the CORe Method is an *action* plan to translate intention into reality, spelling out what will be done that's of concrete benefit to customers. This action plan depicts, in a way that people who'll use it can understand, what actions are to be taken and when, who needs to be involved, what their roles will be, and what resources they'll need.

Avoiding Traditional "Plan" Shortcomings

A "plan" or "proposal" has come to mean a "document." Historically, these were prepared for high-level financial decision making when it was thought that this could be done by remote control through numbers. Much else was messy detail, and implementation was for somebody else—at a lower level—to worry about. Such plans typically focused inside the company and therefore had little to do with customers and only a tenuous connection to bottom-line results.

Traditional plans present a fragmented picture by failing to address how a proposal (a project) fits with day-to-day activities and, therefore, overlooking the full extent of the resources involved. As a result, financial projections are based on incomplete facts. This explains why results so often fall short of expectations: These were false to begin with.

Project proposals usually cover the role of only one or a few—but rarely all—functions or consist of generic implementation phases. The implicit objective is usually to complete the project, the assumption being that financial benefits will then materialize.

By not describing how a resource commitment will add to value for customers and what bottom-line benefits a company can expect, conventional plans leave major questions unanswered. For example:

▲ How does adopting a new inventory control methodology tie in with customers' criteria for deciding which supplier to buy from?

▲ With marketing expenditures factored into the cost of introducing a new product, when will the expected increase in profits occur?

▲ After the purchase of highly automated equipment, what more needs to be done for projected cost reductions to materialize?

Questions like these don't arise when you have a plan of action designed to result in greater value for customers that ties in with marketing activities. Such an action plan shows how bottom-line benefits are to be achieved. The very existence of such a plan also dramatically increases the likelihood that these benefits will be realized.

Preventing Implementation Problems

Sketchy action planning invites implementation difficulties, making disappointing results almost inevitable. Lack of commitment—commonly believed to be the principal cause of disappointing results—is actually a consequence of poor action planning: It's natural to withhold commitment from something if you don't think it will work.

Inadequate action planning caused many companies to find out *after* embarking on extensive efforts to automate manufacturing operations that:

▲ Hoped-for savings in direct labor didn't materialize. In fact, defining how actual labor costs were to be reduced was not required in the investment justification.

▲ Costs associated with adding people skilled in maintaining the new equipment exceeded labor savings.

▲ The time required of people involved in or affected by use of the equipment—shop floor operators and supervisors, materials management personnel—was greater than expected.

▲ Many questions and conflicts arose about the relative priority of working on the automation project, supplying and revising current products, developing new products and markets, and attending to other improvement efforts.

Experienced people know that such issues are likely to arise, making them manageable in advance. The remedy is to have the people involved in realizing results develop a complete and cohesive action plan.

A well-constructed action plan serves several vital uses in addition to guiding implementation. It provides you with a full, factual, and rational foundation for decision making. This foundation makes it possible to:

▲ Make resource allocation decisions with confidence;
▲ Resolve questions about overall priorities *before* they arise;
▲ Define financial targets that all management team members have reason to believe are realistic; and
▲ If necessary, demonstrate convincingly to the people who control funding or approve hiring how certain resource additions are essential to serve customers effectively and profitably. This minimizes debate and second-guessing about plans or proposals.

Such an action plan also serves as a management tool for communicating direction and tracking progress during implementation. Moreover, the process of developing the plan is an opportunity to establish its credibility with the people whose efforts will make the difference between the success and failure of its implementation.

Involving the Key Players in Implementation

The type of action plan developed with the CORe Method is commonly referred to as a time line. It shows the needed actions in a way that everyone, especially the people who'll take them, can easily understand and use.

An organizationwide plan of action cannot be captured on lists of action items, which would be so numerous and so long as to be unworkable. A diagram showing key actions and the connections among them, the major milestones, timing, and responsibilities need not be elaborately detailed or presented. Using sophisticated software isn't necessary (in fact, predetermined formats constrain depiction of a unique action plan). Common understanding is the goal, and a simple, even handwritten diagram—though it lacks elegance—can be the best way to achieve this. A sample layout is shown in Figure 3-7.

The people who put together the action plan should be representative of those who'll be responsible for implementing it. The key players in implementation were identified during Step Two. The continued involvement of these people brings their firsthand knowledge of day-to-day activities to development of the action plan. This speeds the process, produces the best possible action plan, and builds on the sense of ownership initiated in Step Two.

The involvement of someone responsible for marketing activities ensures that these will tie in with action plan timing and, therefore, the time when improved performance for customers becomes a reality. Whether entering a new customer segment, or aiming to advance the company's standing with customers in a segment where it currently does business, taking advantage of the company's enhanced ability to serve customers implies a change in sales and marketing efforts. Whatever the nature of these efforts (customers invited to visit your facilities, new marketing materials, product demonstrations or samples), the resources they involve are part of the foundation needed for sound decisions about resource allocations and for accurate projections of financial results.

Who, specifically, does the action planning varies with the business issues you're facing, the types of changes called for, and at what level in the organization accountability lies. For example:

▲ A company manufacturing nondurable products for consumers needed to reverse poor relationships with current customers who would be key users of a major new product. The necessary changes involved mainly procedures, communication flows, day-to-day responsibilities, and the design and use of a new operating measurement. The people who put the action plan together were drawn from those directly responsible for the supply and revision of current products—mid- and lower-level managers from manufacturing, production planning, order processing, and marketing.

▲ A business unit that made engine parts was defining its longer-term direction and growth plans. Changes involved shaping and focusing the organization to operate as a cohesive whole

Figure 3-7. An extract of an action plan.

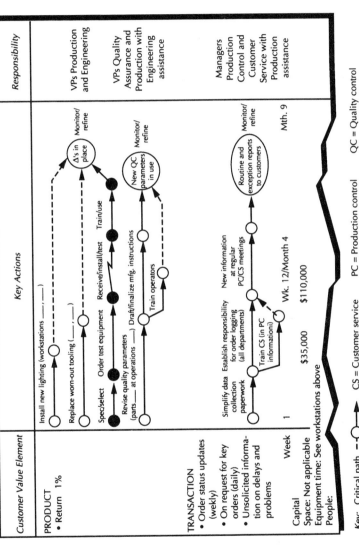

Customer Value Element	Key Actions	Responsibility
PRODUCT • Return 1%	Install new lighting (workstations ——, ——) Replace worn-out tooling (——, ——) Spec/select Order test equipment Receive/install/test Train/use Δ's in place Monitor/refine Revise quality parameters (parts —— at operations ——) Draft/finalize mfg. instructions New QC parameters in use Monitor/refine Train operators	VPs Production and Engineering VPs Quality Assurance and Production with Engineering assistance
TRANSACTION • Order status updates (wekly) • On request for key orders (daily) • Unsolicited information on delays and problems	Simplify data collection Establish responsibility for order logging (all departments) New information at regular PC/CS meetings Routine and exception reports to customers Monitor/refine Train CS (in PC information)	Managers Production Control and Customer Service with Production assistance
Week	1	Wk. 12/Month 4	Mth. 9
Capital	$35,000	$110,000
Space: Not applicable Equipment time: See workstations above People:		

Key: Critical path --○-->   —○—> = Customer service   PC = Production control   QC = Quality control and adding certain people and physical assets. The people who developed the action plan were the division general manager and the vice-presidents who reported to him—the same people who had developed the target market position. Several of these people were closely involved in day-to-day activities; indeed, a key reason for defining the division's direction was so that it could be communicated to middle managers, thereby liberating the executives from having to get deeply involved in firefighting. But despite their familiarity with day-to-day activities, the vice-presidents conferred frequently with people at lower levels when shaping the action plan.

When the senior management team develops the plan, the more they seek input from people lower down the better. Having a say in the action plan lets people see that it doesn't "belong" to any one part of the organization but to the company or business unit as a whole. Should development of the action plan be delegated, management team members must be available for consultation.

Articulating Positive Assumptions

The fact that the action plan has to do with the real world of day-to-day activities, customers, and the company's future prosperity makes action planning inherently worthwhile. Nonetheless, shaping an action plan is challenging work. It requires that you understand and piece together various types of actions, wrestle with what-if and if-then questions, and take the trouble to ensure that the way the plan is depicted on paper is understandable to the people who'll follow it.

As with any planning, uncertainty about the future and concern about repercussions if results don't pan out can cause the people putting the plan together to be overly cautious, particularly if they've been burned before. Laying out certain ground rules for shaping the action plan helps ensure that it's as accurate and believable as possible.

All good plans state the assumptions on which they are based. But many common assumptions are unlikely to be articulated. For example:

▲ Different parts of the organization will continue to work on their own agendas, which will put implementation at cross-purposes and make getting support a hassle.
▲ Needed resources won't be made available.
▲ Whatever management says, its commitment will be absent or short-lived.

Assumed to be inevitable facts of life, such beliefs usually result in built-in conservatism.

Customary roadblocks to implementation have bred skepticism, causing action planning to be viewed as just another well-intentioned but academic exercise. This skepticism is based on the premise that implementation will be relegated to desirable-but-optional status, meaning that initial enthusiasm will fizzle into excuses and people will distance themselves from an effort that cannot succeed. Such perceptions cause experienced people developing a plan to pad it and those approving a plan to allow for the "fudge factor"—discounting stated resource requirements and raising projected benefits. This self-perpetuating cycle means that no one—neither planners nor approvers—knows for sure what actions and results are really intended and what time and resources are really needed.

Articulating positive assumptions helps counteract skepticism and padding and dispel doubts about the seriousness of action planning. Although a level of uncertainty is inevitable when dealing with the future, stating explicit assumptions confirms and reinforces that this time the planning effort is for real. These positive assumptions have to do with support, priorities, and resources. Here's how one general manager worded the assumptions to the group of people developing the action plan:

▲ Customer-oriented changes directly impact both short-term results and the company's future welfare. I will take a hands-on role in guiding the work required to accomplish these changes. I intend to monitor progress and give you the support you need. This includes intervening on your behalf when necessary.
▲ Advancing the company's standing with customers—that is, work on this action plan—will have top priority day in and day out.

▲ Resources called for by the action plan will be provided to the greatest extent possible. If it turns out that specific resources are not available, I will let you know so you can revise the plan accordingly.

Replacing commonly unstated negative assumptions with ones that are explicit and positive produces an action plan that will work in the same way that concentrated efforts in special circumstances do. Examples of such instances are:

▲ Recapturing, through a concerted effort by people in various parts of the organization, what appears to be a lost order
▲ Completing production in time to ship before Christmas shutdown by using nonstandard equipment or having managers help out on the shop floor

Devising the Shortest Route to Improved Results

The customer value element or elements that requires action to attain a target market position drive development of the action plan. Specific product and service attributes indicate which of the approaches to accomplish customer-oriented changes (defined in Step Two—Concreteness: Scoping Out Needed Changes) belong in the action plan. In keeping with the way the approaches were developed, *what* is to be done comes before *who* is to do it.

Since the time for each action is already known (identified in Step Two), the principal dates are easy to determine. Laying out, sequentially over time, the actions needed to address all aspects of implementation and how these actions connect reveals the milestones along the way to the target market position. For example, revising current products to meet customers' needs requires finding vendors and receiving materials before pilot manufacture can start. Subsequently, draft manufacturing processes and quality assurance procedures can be revised and completed. A milestone along this path would therefore be satisfactory completion of pilot manufacture, with documentation approved. Production of initial finished goods inventory would then lead to a major milestone: introduction of the revised product, which would be followed by a period of monitoring customer acceptance and experience with the new product. Longer-term activities, such as new product development or licensing of products or technology to fill customers' unmet needs, would proceed concurrently with work on product revisions and have their own milestones, such as availability of prototypes for initial customer trials.

Milestones that are too few, too big, and too far apart seem remote, lack meaning, and may appear unattainable. For example, introducing five product revisions and one new product within twelve months can seem overwhelming, whereas an intermediate goal of introducing three revisions within six months looks more manageable. More, smaller, and shorter-term goals also keep up the momentum: Achieving each one produces a sense of accomplishment, builds confidence, and encourages efforts to tackle the next one.

Precision in setting dates for achievement of milestones isn't necessary. Time periods counted in weeks or months in the shorter-term and then in quarters, or even years, are accurate enough. As time goes by, dates can and should be set more precisely.

Workable Shortcuts. Identifying the tasks that add up to the critical path indicates where it might be possible to compress overall timing. Reviewing the time line with the people who defined and will actually perform the tasks can reveal what are, in their judgment, workable shortcuts. This might call for a more detailed time line for a section of the overall action plan in order to identify shortcuts that are feasible and not unwise. For example, making a preliminary, informal submission to regulatory authorities for their initial comments, to be reflected in final documentation submitted formally, could avoid two cycles of the statutory review-and-response time.

Any alternative approaches defined in Step Two—Concreteness: Scoping Out Needed Changes can also be considered as ways to compress timing, possibly at additional cost. A revised product could be ready for market sooner by subcontracting manufacture of initial quantities while you gear up for in-house manufacturer. Having outside specialists help get new software up and running and conduct training could shorten the time until provision of full, prompt, and accurate response to customer inquiries is a reality.

Start Dates for Minor Tasks. Although actions that determine overall timing are most crucial, setting start dates for secondary tasks guards against their being a cause of unnecessary delays. Working backwards from a milestone shows when the smaller tasks, such as preparations to announce an improved product or a simpler pricing structure, are to start. Actions preparatory to such an announcement may all be standard procedure, but their completion must coincide with the major milestone.

Actions related to seemingly minor tasks can appear too detailed to warrant identification in the organization's overall time line. But failure to set start dates for secondary tasks risks their dictating the rate of progress. If people responsible for minor tasks are taken by surprise, they will have to engage others in a disorderly—and possibly costly—scramble to catch up. And the efforts of the people who accomplished major tasks on time will appear to be undervalued.

Seeking Key Players' Buy-In

The people putting the action plan together were selected because they will have key roles in implementation. Their—and others'—specific roles have yet to be defined. Some people will welcome the chance to show what they can do in a leadership role and to be accountable, but others might not feel ready to take responsibility for producing results of significance to the whole organization. The people who developed the action plan probably have suggestions about roles, that is, who is to be the leader, who else is to be on a team, and who else needs to be available for counsel.

Reviewing the time line with a cross section of people who'll be involved in putting the plan into practice—people other than those who developed it—serves to sound them out about the roles they are ready and willing to take. This review, conducted when the action plan is close to its final form, serves other purposes. It verifies that the time line is complete and accurate, gives the people who'll use it a chance to get familiar with the format, and helps sustain their sense of participation. Seeing the action itself makes people aware that change is really on the way, not just under discussion.

Aggregating Total Resource Requirements

Since the action plan encompasses all functions, resource requirements are for the company as a whole, not just for certain functions or departments or for a distinct program. With actions laid out in the time line and the associated resources already identified in Step Two, compiling resource requirements consists of listing them according to when they are needed and for how long. As in Step Two, the resource categories are people's time, equipment and space, and money (working capital and, possibly, investment capital).

Some actions require only people's time, perhaps on a part-time basis for a limited period. Thus, people from production planning, marketing, and data processing might get started immediately on improving forecast accuracy for reliable delivery and work intensively for a few weeks. As this effort tapers off, marketing would then work with finance to redesign sales promotion programs in keeping with customer order patterns. And, possibly in parallel, technical service people might work with sales for a few weeks to set up files of customers' product-use experience and then work with people who answer the telephone, providing training and developing paperwork for handling and documenting customer calls.

Other actions call for a full-time effort by some people as well as dedicated space and equipment at certain times. Product development, manufacturing, and purchasing people might be needed to work full time on product revisions; they would require space to work as a group and computer time for a few months. They would then need to involve shop-floor operators and have the use of dedicated manufacturing equipment. During the weeks when the revised product is being field-tested, demand on the time of shop-floor people and equipment would drop; it would then increase again for the making of refinements before phasing over to commercial production. Computer time would also be needed by order processing and finance people working to put a stop to billing problems. And access to certain manufacturing equipment would be required for work on reducing set-up time or scrap and rework and for testing a new maintenance program.

Working capital needs are also extracted from the time line. These include building inventory before product launch, engaging specialized outside expertise in the short term, subcontracting with manufacturers for certain product components, paying for the higher cost of more frequent shipments, funding travel to develop relationships with new customers, and buying marketing materials for a new market area or space near customers' locations.

When mid-level managers are compiling the resource requirements, they may need help from people in finance when determining working capital needs. For all types of resources, however, projections need not be precise to the last hour or dollar. Estimates based on a thorough job of action planning are innately more accurate than figures correct to the fourth decimal place that are based on superficial planning.

Minimum Resource Additions. The action plan inherently minimizes the need for additional resources. It is aimed at the specific changes needed to attain a target market position and consists of tailored approaches to accomplish these changes. Both the market position and these approaches were designed expressly to build on the company's current strengths and capabilities. This means that the action plan takes advantage of existing resources to the greatest extent possible, such as by adding a shift (instead of building or acquiring a new facility) or providing skills training for current employees (rather than hiring new people).

Resource additions to increase capacity may be unnecessary. Once customer-oriented changes and ongoing activities that produce value for customers take priority over other work, less time and energy go to nonessential activities. Whether an increase in capacity is called for and worthwhile will be ascertained later when determining how best to allocate resources.

Whether customer-oriented changes are to strengthen performance in a segment you currently serve or prepare for entry into a new one, resource additions identified at this stage are only those crucial to providing superior value—as called for in the target market position—and to take advantage of it through sales and marketing activities. These additions would be used to gain specific knowledge, skills, or capabilities that cannot be developed in-house or when acquiring them offers a significant time advantage. Such instances include:

▲ The purchase of equipment to handle parts or materials that your current equipment cannot, or the purchase of computer capabilities your current hardware lacks;
▲ The hiring of a person with top-flight experience in running an after-sales service operation, who's skilled in developing sales promotion programs for certain end users or who's expert in the application of a particular technology; and
▲ The acquisition of another company's products to supplement yours, so that you can offer certain customers the broader line or one-stop shopping they seek.

The need for capital investment varies with the types of issues, the actions needed to resolve them, and the time span involved. Cementing a strong position in a customer segment you currently serve (e.g., by making minor changes to product packaging or refining current delivery performance) may require no capital investment. However, more radical changes—to advance from a so-so status with customers to that of a preferred supplier—might need new capital, such as:

▲ Major product configuration changes requiring a particular piece of equipment you currently lack;
▲ Prompt and full response to customers' questions about product availability by providing the order processing department or sales reps with more sophisticated computer terminals that connect to the mainframe; and
▲ Significant reduction of manufacturing lead time that calls for additional tooling or materials handling equipment.

When new funding is required, the further in the future the requirement, the less precise the figures need be. This minimizes the time spent on number crunching.

Whatever the amount and whenever it's called for, the fact that new funding will enable the company to provide specific products or services that are highly significant to customers gives you a compelling rationale for making the investment. Investing to

build the company's capabilities for *customer* advantage is investing in the ultimate source of return: customers in a segment known
to be a significant profit generator that therefore offers the best
prospects of high returns. Moreover, justifying capital investment
on the basis of performance in customers' eyes, which relates
directly to higher revenue and profits, avoids having to wait until
costs are so high as to justify investment based on savings.

▲   ▲   ▲

Now that the action plan has been mapped out and the timing
of all resource requirements extracted from it, the senior management team has a solid foundation on which to base resource
allocation decisions. These are made in the next part of Step Three.

Part C: Resources for Customers, Profits for the Company

*You define how changes to provide superior value for customers will fit
with current activities. Based on the customer segment or segments to be
focused on, the target market position, and the action plan, you redefine
resource allocations in light of overall priorities. You then project
financial results and agree on bottom-line targets. Part C is highlighted
in Figure 3-8.*

▲   ▲   ▲

Accomplishment of customer-oriented changes in an ongoing
business is not a separate undertaking but one that people
throughout the company or business unit will take part in or be
affected by. Superimposing an action plan on current activities and
hoping for the best leaves it up to people at lower levels to call the
shots about priorities. This means that current priorities are likely
to continue, favoring business as usual.

With a new direction defined and the customer-oriented
changes it calls for spelled out, current priorities become outdated.
Aligning resource allocations and overall priorities with that new
direction will make planned action part of the mainstream. As an

Figure 3-8. Step Three—The Crux: Establishing the New Direction, Part C.

A	B	C	D	E
Which Customers? How to Attract and Keep Them?	**Blueprint for Action**	**Resources for Customers, Profits for the Company**	**Setting the Stage**	**Management Team Sanction**
Customer Segment to Focus on	Time-Phased Action Plan	Decisions on: —Resource Allocations	Definition of Key Organizational Adjustments	Review and Agreement
Target Market Position	Key Players Resources Needed	—Overall Priorities —Financial Targets		Formal Approvals

Step One Understanding Customer Viewpoints →

Step Two Scoping Out Needed Changes →

Step Four Working Together for Customers and Profits

integral part of day-to-day activities, providing superior value for customers will get the level of attention it deserves. How resources are allocated among customer-oriented changes, everyday activities, and any other projects provides a complete foundation on which to project profitability and investment returns. In turn, accurate projections make it possible to set realistic financial targets. And seeing that targeted results are attainable encourages commitment to realize them.

Making Customer Orientation the Top Priority

The likelihood of priority clashes among day-to-day activities and projects is already considerable. Simply adding customer-oriented changes to the list would exacerbate the situation, increasing the choices and the chances of counterproductive resolutions. Only when guided by one set of overall business priorities that incorporates and emphasizes customers can a company operate cohesively and provide superior value. However, stating overall priorities that highlight orientation to customers is not enough. Resource allocations have to reflect this emphasis also.

The target market position is almost certain to call for reallocation of resources. Recasting overall resource allocations, in turn, makes the current operating plan obsolete. Failure to recast departmental budgets accordingly can cause planned action to get sidetracked.

Building Unanimity Among Top Management

All organizations suffer to some degree from forces that work against innovation. The more established a company, the greater the built-in bias against change is likely to be. Founded in times when demand could be taken for granted—when inward focus on resource control to maximize efficiency was the name of the game—older companies tend to have more, clearer cut internal jurisdictions. Even in a smaller, younger organization there's a natural tendency for its parts (hierarchical levels, functions, departments, existing teams) to drift apart and go their separate ways. Knitting those parts together into a cohesive whole—an organization that operates like a well-oiled machine producing superior value for customers and outstanding financial results—is something that only senior management can do.

Clearly, only senior management can—or should—set overall priorities and decide on resource allocations, additions, and bottom-line targets. But when even one functional head is excluded from deliberations on these matters, he or she is likely to lack confidence in the viability of the whole undertaking and conviction in its chances for success. This makes generating broad commitment lower down in the organization highly unlikely.

Any lack of senior management support will be easily and quickly detected, and it can be infectious. Introducing planned action in a lukewarm way or distancing oneself from it (here's the plan, now you implement it) invites negative response. Buy-in is voluntary and based not just on feelings (a sense of involvement) but also on reason and self-interest. Every person on the management team must therefore have the opportunity to use his or her judgment to determine whether the action plan is workable and the hoped-for results attainable and worth striving for.

Establishing the management team members' faith in the action plan—and, consequently, building their commitment to achieve the targeted results—starts with allocating resources to meet the requirements laid out in the plan. A mismatch between resources acquired and those assigned is a valid reason to doubt that an action plan is workable and to withhold commitment to its success. The aim is therefore to determine how best to reallocate resources, looking at existing resources first. This can be a touchy subject, but it's something of an acid test. If people at the top of the company or business unit can't find a way to pull together, it's unreasonable to expect people at lower levels to do so.

Allocating Resources to Customers First

Based on the resource requirements extracted from the action plan, you can determine where implementation is likely to cause an overload on resources as currently allocated. In most cases, work on the action plan will be in addition to work on current projects and regular duties. Identifying where and when overloads are likely to arise indicates where tasks need to be reassigned or resources reallocated.

The product and service attributes that matter most to high-potential customer segments have the strongest claim on existing resources. Conversely, any customer segment designated as not worth investing in has a weak claim. Any decrease in the attention paid to such a segment—and, by implication, any products or services that apply only to it—frees the time of people and equipment to work on changes for customers in more important segments.

Projects or programs initiated in the past that lack relevance to customers can also be a source of resources. Product development projects are one place to look for efforts that are of little significance to customers in an important customer segment. Refining product development efforts and the scope of operational improvement programs ensures that they focus where they will have the greatest impact. For example:

▲ The resources required by the action plan to work on set-up time reduction to smooth manufacturing flow and speed delivery might be made available by simply cutting back on meetings and paperwork associated with current improvement programs.

▲ Calling a halt to efforts to make minor cost reductions, such as using cheaper packaging materials, could free the time of technical people who are needed to provide customers with a higher level of postsale support.

Supporters of projects and programs already under way might be less than enthusiastic about cutbacks, but they will probably recognize the wisdom of a tighter, more customer-oriented focus.

Reviewing past decisions about resource additions can also free resources for customer-oriented changes. A new budget slot or an approved funding—earmarked for purposes in line with yesterday's priorities—might be used differently than originally intended.

Revising approved resource additions is not likely to be popular, but the point is not which function or department gets the largest slice of the pie. It is to determine how best to allocate the resources of the company as a whole to key customer segments and the product and service attributes that matter most to them.

One department may "lose" and another "gain," but keeping resource additions to a minimum is of benefit to the entire company.

Reallocations must not, of course, detract from activities related to product and service attributes that customers value but that do not need improvement and are therefore not covered in the action plan. If resources are taken from such activities, the current level of performance will not be maintained.

Prioritizing Other Activities

The concept of putting 80 percent of your resources to work for the 20 percent of customers who provide 80 percent of your profits is a proper guideline when defining overall direction. That concept is also a proper starting point to make resource allocation decisions. However, when making these decisions, topics of more significance to the company than to customers directly also come into the picture. Such topics include:

▲ Environmental, regulatory, and legal matters;
▲ Matters related to employees' welfare, such as providing a safe and presentable working environment;
▲ Cost reductions that affect margins, not pricing; and
▲ Issues related to the company's social responsibility, such as support for community efforts to improve education.

Stipulating the customer- or company-related topics that have high organizationwide priority is only half the battle. You must also specify the projects and topics whose priority is to drop. This underscores the point that yesterday's narrow and inward focus is a thing of the past.

A way to look at other projects and topics is in terms of whom they benefit and their meaning for the company and its results. Figure 3-9 provides a frame of reference for considering the relative priority of topics that aren't directly related to serving customers.

As a general rule, work associated with maintaining or increasing value delivered to customers must come first, although customer-oriented changes may not take precedence on any given day. The priority assigned to any particular topic or activity not

Figure 3-9. A framework for setting priorities.

Priority	Key Beneficiary	Activity Set	Impact
1	Customers	Changes to add to value delivered Ongoing delivery of value	Make progress and make money
2	Customers indirectly and the company	Employee relations Cost reductions for wider margins Basic research Investment decisions/financing	Manage resources and save money
3	Company only	Tax, legal, and regulatory matters Community relations	Avoid trouble and avoid cost

directly related to serving customers can only be judged and adjusted by senior management.

Writing down the management team's conclusions about what falls within each priority set is essential. This record of overall business priorities will be used to communicate direction at the outset of implementation and as a reference to guide managers in making day-to-day decisions and solving problems.

Even with overall priorities clarified, decisions on resource allocations are likely to involve trade-offs. Therefore, iteration is almost inevitable. However, a shortfall in resources allocated to the action plan must be avoided so as not to jeopardize the projected rate of progress being realized. If a resource shortfall is unavoidable, the action plan must be revised.

Projecting the Bottom-Line Benefit

Working with the action plan timeline and the resource decisions just made, you can project realistically the amount and timing of financial impacts. Although accounting conventions vary from company to company, calculating the bottom-line benefit starts with determining the net impact of the various components of revenues and costs. It's tempting to guess ahead at the net impact on profits but, given the interplay between revenues and costs as affected by decisions made so far in this step, accurate estimates are close to impossible. For example, an increase in unit volume from customers purchasing customized products (good news) would reduce somewhat the volume in standard products (bad news); higher prices for customized products imply higher gross margins (good news); and the related selling and support costs might be higher (bad news) or lower (good news), although no finished goods inventory is needed (good news).

The Revenue Impact. Revenue will be affected sometime after performance improvement becomes a reality. Knowledge of the customer viewpoint in the targeted segment, which you gained in Step One, helps determine at what rate revenue is likely to increase there. In general, sales revenue from customers who make frequent purchases will increase faster than from those who purchase products rarely, are dissatisfied with the performance of all suppliers, or for whom you're making a particular innovation that offers them outstanding benefits. For example, a company supplying auto parts bought its own trucks, which enabled it to deliver to customers whenever they needed. Customers quickly shifted the bulk of their purchases to this company (other suppliers remained at the mercy of railroad or trucking company schedules), producing an early and sizable increase in its sales revenue.

Customers you currently do business with will notice the improvements in your company's performance. Nonetheless, even current customers may want to wait to make sure that this performance is sustained before increasing the volume of business they do with your company. And the good news about your superior performance will travel. New customers are also likely to take their time, however, issuing small sample orders to see whether the superiority you claim is real before switching suppliers.

Determining the revenue impact also entails a review of customary allowances for discounts and returns. A drop in returns as quality improves, or as overstocking decreases once sales promotion programs are restructured to suit customer buying patterns, implies a decrease in those allowances. Revenue impact may also have to be netted if, for example, sales of certain products through a new channel cannibalize current sales through another.

The Cost Impact. The overall cost impact is also the result of several factors and is likely to be gradual. Few actions cause an immediate drop in costs. As with revenue, the beneficial impact on costs is driven by accomplishment of changes covered in the action plan. For example, only when a product redesigned for ease of use is in customers' hands will the costs of providing in-use technical support decrease.

Costs related to serving customers in a particular segment or to supplying certain products might actually increase. When these higher costs are for reallocated resources, there is no impact on the bottom line. This is also the case when reapportioning overheads through an accounting change—allocating to a customer segment only those overheads associated with doing business there—to track more accurately profits generated in that segment.

Since everything possible has already been done to minimize resource additions, any projected cost increases are deliberate and desirable. Possible cost increases include overtime for current employees instead of using temporary help or hiring; write-offs of residual inventory to get improved products into customers' hands earlier; cash outlays that speed implementation action, such as outside expertise to provide training in computer usage; and hiring to acquire specific knowledge and skills, or acquiring equipment with particular capabilities that the company lacks but must have to provide superior value to customers.

Agreeing on Bottom-Line Targets

How soon you can expect profit gains to materialize varies with the issues being addressed. Action to effect a change in long-term direction probably means a later profit impact. For example, focusing on high-volume accounts that buy directly rather than on multiple small wholesalers might cause no short-term change in unit volumes and in the sum of selling, marketing, distribution, and field service costs. But as direct buyers switch their business to your company and their share of end-user demand increases, revenues can be expected to increase faster than in the past, despite pricing at volume discounts. At the same time, related sales, general, and administrative costs can be expected to drop as a percentage of each sales dollar. This would net out to a minimal, if any, bottom-line increase in the short term but significantly higher profitability beyond that.

The projected profit increase may be a pleasant surprise. For example, a company making nondurable products for consumers was setting out to improve delivery performance and resolve relationship problems with distributors. After a matter of months, a modest price increase, a slight increase in unit volume, and avoidance of costs associated with delivery delays (such as picking up shipping costs usually paid by customers) were projected to convert a shortfall into a more than 15 percent increase over past profitability. Another company, supplying the defense industry, defined its overall direction for the first time and found that new projections of net operating profit exceeded current ones by 10 percent for the next year and by 25 percent for the succeeding three years. The increases would result from more business in the current market area, once resource additions were in place and other needed changes bore fruit, and then—starting in eighteen months—from first orders from customers in a new segment.

Whatever the amount and rate of the projected profit increase, testing its sensitivity to key variables helps build confidence in the numbers. Thus, for any key drivers of profitability, recalculating the projections based on an optimistic and a pessimistic figure reveals how sensitive the bottom-line figures are. The management team can then decide on the projections that are realistic and appropriately ambitious.

One question remains before projected results can be considered targets: How close do these projections come to the company's stated objectives? Comparing the company's financial objectives—x percent operating profit, y percent annual growth, z percent return on invested capital—with projected results indicates whether earlier decisions need to be revised.

Given the quality of the information and the rigorous reasoning used to arrive at these projections, the chances of raising them by working through a further iteration may seem slim. But it may be worthwhile to do so, even though it implies taking resources away from what you consider to be important topics.

Reducing support for topics of mostly internal significance could obviate the need to take any resources away from activities directly associated with serving customers. However, if absolutely unavoidable, taking resources away from the product and services attributes that matter least in a customer segment with low profit potential will be least harmful in both the short and long run.

▲   ▲   ▲

Having decided on resource allocations, restated overall priorities as necessary, and set financial targets, you've reached what's usually considered the end of the planning cycle. Implementation would follow directly. However, assuming that implementation will not encounter any organizational impediments risks finding out about them too late—when action to accomplish needed changes has already foundered. Identifying organizational hurdles to successful implementation therefore comes next.

Part D: Setting the Stage

In light of the overall direction and priorities defined earlier in this step, you review the organizational infrastructure—roles and responsibilities, the organizational structure, business performance measurements, and the reward system—and make adjustments as needed to foster orientation to customers and bottom-line results. Part D is highlighted in Figure 3-10.

▲   ▲   ▲

Perceived as signifying what senior management deems most important, the messages sent by the organizational infrastructure carry great weight. Any aspect of the infrastructure that is inconsistent with serving customers and producing profits will be confusing to people lower down in the organization. These mixed signals are powerful and insidious hurdles to successful implementation of the action plan.

With direction in customers' terms defined, the action plan mapped out, and overall priorities restated, you can examine the current infrastructure in a new light. Making selected adjustments ensures that all aspects of the infrastructure are properly aligned and sending clear, consistent, and results-oriented signals to

Figure 3-10. Step Three—The Crux: Establishing the New Direction, Part D.

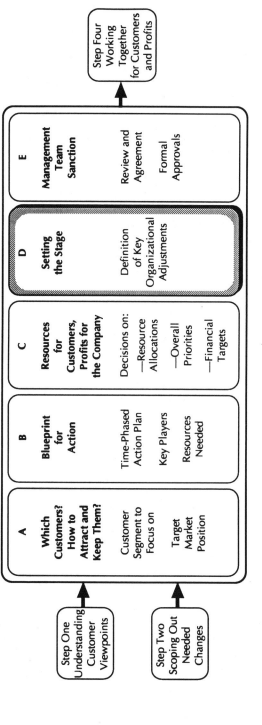

people at all levels and in all functions. A properly aligned organizational infrastructure also reinforces senior management's leadership, getting orientation to customers and bottom-line targets entrenched as early, fully, and firmly as possible.

Accommodating Results-Oriented Action

There are only two vantage points from which to see the organization as a whole: the customers' vantage point and the one from the top of the organization.

Certain adjustments to your organization and management mechanisms have been defined in the action plan, but the whole infrastructure must tie in with them. For example, a person who is accountable for leading efforts to attain a particular milestone is certain to run into difficulties when someone else thinks that accountability is his or hers. Roles and areas of responsibility would need to be adjusted. And a new operational measurement based on the customer viewpoint is likely to be ignored when it conflicts with historical departmental measures used—or perceived to be used—to evaluate people's performance. The reward system would need adjusting to be consistent with the new measurement.

Addressing organizational matters can be a touchy subject, however. Many people have firm convictions about what's right, especially about organizational structure, and they may not coincide. Structural changes—who reports to whom—have implications about territory and status. How business performance is measured and individual performance rewarded are also sensitive issues. There's always the temptation to try to come up with arrangements that are just right for everyone.

There's no such thing as an organizational infrastructure that's *right*. There is no perfect model. However, there are ways in which roles and responsibilities, the structure itself, business performance measurements, and the reward system can clearly be *wrong*—that is, at odds with the company's direction and priorities and the actions and behaviors these call for.

The main objective is to correct aspects of the current infrastructure that will cause implementation of customer-oriented changes to falter and therefore keep a target market position from being attained.

Redefining Roles and Responsibilities

Most companies have strict do's and don'ts about roles and responsibilities, many of which make no sense. People therefore go outside the rules—as they should. For example, someone in manufacturing isn't supposed to have direct contact with customers, but he bends the rule and picks up the telephone to give a customer the information he needs.

Identifying needed adjustments in roles and responsibilities—of functions, departments, individuals, and levels in the hierarchy—comes first. How the organization operates is more important than how it is structured. The form-follows-function principle applies. At a company that makes health care products—and is known for its consistently strong financial performance—structure is considered so unimportant that there is no organization chart. The reasoning is that such a chart sends the wrong messages, such as:

▲ People belong in little boxes.
▲ Bosses—the boxes at the top of the chart—are inherently most important.
▲ The scope and nature of individual responsibilities can be fully and accurately defined in advance.

These messages are directly opposed to the characteristics of that organization. There, people at all levels are expected to think broadly and to take the initiative when they detect something that needs attending to. Unusually high collaboration among departments and levels is the norm.

Another characteristic is a strong sense of individual responsibility for results. How a person at any level performs his or her job, which includes seeking his or her boss's counsel when in doubt, is up to the individual rather than limited by a job description. While your company may not be ready to do away with the organization chart and job descriptions, certain roles and responsibilities may need to be adjusted for greater orientation to customers. Adjustments to roles and responsibilities are preferable to structural changes; they cause less anxiety and disruption.

Roles and responsibilities redefined to highlight delivery of value to customers can be a radical departure from historical definitions, which typically emphasized departmental scope and tight control for efficiency. For example, manufacturing's traditional role has been to maximize output and minimize cost. By implication, this discouraged attention to product quality, materials flow, nonstandard production, and joint efforts with other departments and functions. If manufacturing's role isn't redefined to reflect changes called for in the action plan, the discrepancy could hinder implementation.

Redefining the nature of certain managerial roles might also be needed. Less emphasis on being the boss and more emphasis on leading and helping with collaborative customer-oriented changes might be in order. For example, when salespeople and technical personnel are to work together to develop relationships with new customers, the sales manager's role might need to be revised to deemphasize insistence on a certain number of sales calls per day and instead assist in preparing for visits to customers.

Responsibilities defined in terms of product categories can impede customer orientation. Realigning responsibilities at the customer interface (e.g., in sales, order processing, and field service) to suit customers is therefore logical and would probably be covered in the action plan. For example, reassigning the responsibilities of salespeople according to customer segments would remove an irritation for customers: having to deal with multiple salespeople from the same company. Redefining responsibilities within marketing along the same lines makes for consistency. Such redefinition can usefully broaden and elevate the marketing manager's or project manager's role, injecting greater orientation to customers and profitability into day-to-day activities, including interactions with other departments.

Such redefinitions can seem burdensome but make good sense. Having the same people from different parts of the organization work together routinely speeds communication and strengthens working relationships both internally and with customers. People throughout the organization will know who is the internal expert on a particular customer segment and go to him or her for the latest and best information. In addition, accountability for profitability in a certain customer segment is clarified.

A marketing or product manager whose role is defined in terms of a customer segment becomes the internal spokesperson for customers there and the organization's primary guardian of the profits that segment generates. Such a role provides an excellent training ground for that manager to advance to a higher position: It involves aspects of general management but on a smaller scale. However, even with the requisite knowledge, skills, and experience, effectively performing such a role in marketing is tough to do when other parts of the organization are still oriented strictly along functional lines.

Reshaping the Organizational Structure Around Customers

Using distinctions among customer types to define responsibilities at the customer interface and one stage further into the organization, such as in marketing and finished goods warehousing, is possible without structural changes. But this may not be the case with other functions.

A theoretical ideal, which focuses all functions outward on customers, is to have an entire business unit serve just one customer segment. However, one segment is rarely sufficiently large, stable, and growing to risk tying the existence of a business unit to it. Yet having a single business unit focus on multiple customer segments can be unworkable, with all the drawbacks of bigness and complexity, including elaborate coordination, lengthy communication channels, unwieldy decision making, and lack of awareness of customers and of attention to bottom-line profitability.

Adopting the internal-customer concept—in which departments or divisions make up a chain serving others in the same company—is a sign that a business unit is too big, with too few people answerable for profitability. This concept risks real customers getting lost in the shuffle. Unified focus on external customers works best.

Somewhere between the two extremes of an entire business unit serving only one customer segment or a mammoth business unit serving multiple segments are structures that are both work-able and economically sound. Again, the form-follows-function principle is a sound one. Applying it to organizational structure implies shaping the organization around customers.

Rather than forming a new business unit, which would take months to design and implement and cause major distractions and nervousness, incremental changes can be made. An interim mea-sure toward establishing a new business unit would be defining a "business within the business" that shares certain staff functions. An even less dramatic change would be adjusting certain reporting relationships within the existing business unit. For example, one company had the people in R&D who were involved in customer-oriented changes—product revisions and the later stages of new product development—become part of the manufacturing depart-ment.

In manufacturing, resources are often shared as much as possible to take advantage of economies of scale. Thus, a single manufacturing facility might serve many customer segments, which end up competing with one another for the company's resources. Setting up, within the same facility, distinct manufac-turing operations that focus on certain customer segments is a happy medium between orientation to customers and scale econ-omies. Accordingly, one company split its manufacturing opera-tions and promoted two department managers to directors of manufacturing, reporting to the vice-president of operations. One part of the factory supplies products packed in bulk for further processing by its customers (manufacturers), and the other sup-plies products in finished form for resale by its customers (distrib-utors). Each manufacturing area has its own space, equipment, labor pool, scheduling, purchasing, set-up mechanics, and ware-housing. The quality assurance department has two parts, one for each factory within the factory, and reports directly to the vice-president of operations. Both areas share staff support, such as facilities maintenance, data processing, finance, and personnel.

It's impossible to predict what structural adjustments, if any, your organization might need and how far and how fast you will proceed. But some reshaping around the key customer segments prevents internal boundaries from impeding the company's ability to deliver superior value.

Emphasizing Customer-Oriented
Performance Measurements

From management's perspective, business performance measurements supplement qualitative information garnered from observation and discussion. These measurements have two basic
purposes. First, they serve as indicators, allowing you to know
what's going on, to tell whether things are under control, and to
track progress toward targeted results. In this sense, the measurement system is like the readings displayed on an equipment
control panel: It provides continuous information. The second
purpose of business performance measurements is to provide
input to the reward system. Certain readings from the control
panel indicate whether reward and recognition—or the opposite—
are warranted. Confusion between the two purposes is common
and detrimental: Unless there are clear indications to the contrary,
people will assume that their individual performance evaluations
are based on the measurements that are taken for tracking purposes.

Improving a measurement system is not a simple task, but
having a target market position, overall priorities, and financial
targets based on them makes the task easier—and more worthwhile. For example:

▲ Rather than rely on measurements of resource efficiency,
  you can track overall effectiveness in providing value for
  customers.
▲ Rather than use measurements that show improvement
  compared to the past, you can track progress toward targets.
▲ Rather than have the measurement system imply that everything measured is equally important, you can highlight
  the key measurements. These are, of course, the ones that
  indicate how well the whole company or business unit is
  performing for customers and progressing toward bottom-
  line targets.

Highlighting measurements related to organizationwide performance can mean a radical, positive change in the signals

historically sent and received. When inwardly oriented and localized measurements are perceived to be the most important, attaining them is likely to take precedence over serving customers. Such
measurements include the number of sales calls or amount of
product made each day, purchased materials cost, and line-by-line
budget variances. When action to serve customers is taken and the
numbers are massaged, you receive distorted information. This
defeats the purpose of taking the measurements in the first place.

The principal shortcoming of traditional measurements is
preoccupation with resource consumption relative to outputs. This
preoccupation glosses over, or bypasses entirely, the activities that
drive resource consumption, affecting not only the amount of
output but also other outcomes. Most traditional operational
measurements—reflecting their roots in accounting—emphasize
quantity over quality, localized efficiency over companywide effectiveness, and cost containment for wider margins over value
received by customers.

When you're aiming to maximize output any improvement is
inherently good and more is inherently better. But with sophisticated customers who have a choice among high-performing suppliers, it's crucial to measure how well the company performs for
customers. This calls for operational measurements that focus on
the activities driving that performance. The measurements must
provide the information needed by the people whose actions
translate into value for customers. With prompt feedback on their
actions, people at lower levels can catch and fix potential problems
early—long before they affect customers—and promptly investigate how to prevent recurrence. Having measurements taken by
the people responsible for the activities that drive them reinforces
a sense of responsibility and avoids wasting time on explanation,
debate, and finger pointing, which take time away from work that
produces superior value for customers.

Measuring what drives delivery of value to customers ties in
directly with what the company is setting out to do: achieve a target
market position through a combination of customer-oriented
changes and ongoing activities.

Since what's measured is understood to be what matters to
management, measuring what drives delivery of value to customers reinforces the new direction and overall priorities, namely:

▲ The customer segments to be focused on;
▲ The product and service attributes that matter most to customers and are crucial to the company's target market position; and
▲ Delivery of value to customers now and in the future as the primary concern, before topics of significance only to the company itself.

Measurements that highlight collaborative customer-oriented action send the right message, and they imply that people taking such action are making a significant contribution.

A whole new measurement system isn't necessary and can take months of intense effort. Revising existing measurements as needed is enough to provide the key information you need. By adjusting existing measurements, you make delivery of value to customers a built-in part of the regular course of doing business.

When customer-oriented and current measurements are at cross-purposes, there are three possible adjustments:

1. Redefine a current measurement for companywide or business-unit scope instead of narrower functional or accounting definitions;
2. Reclassify a measurement as secondary or taken for tracking purposes only; or
3. Stop taking the measurement altogether. At one company, a decades-old practice of measuring the output on each shift was simply dropped.

A few easily understandable measurements are enough to indicate business performance. At one company, the management team of the JKL division decided to track and assess performance with five key measurements—four operational and one financial. All five are supported by secondary measurements and differ considerably from measurements taken in the past. For example, the principal operational measurement used to be "productivity," a measurement of efficiency based on the amount of time each machine was working on parts. Manufacturing alone was responsible for meeting or missing that measurement, although it had no control over most of the factors driving the measurement. The productivity measurement signaled that keeping machines busy was the main goal, regardless of customer need dates and regardless of the proportion of parts produced that needed rework or had to be scrapped. The productivity measurement was perceived to imply that products and equipment mattered more than customers and employees. It also implied that other departments' activities had no bearing on productivity.

All operational measurements now apply to the whole of the JKL division: sales and marketing, manufacturing, engineering and plant maintenance, quality control, materials management and purchasing, finance, data processing, and personnel. *Customer-oriented operational measurements* at JKL are of quality (a redefined measurement) and of delivery (a new measurement). Both embody the customer perspective. Delivery performance is measured in terms of the actual shipping date compared with the date last requested by customers. Quality means that finished products are measured against customer specifications. These measurements are taken for tracking purposes and as quantitative input to the reward system.

As called for in the action plan, materials management compiles the measurement of delivery performance, and shop-floor operators take and document measurements of in-process quality. (The quality control department used to be responsible for measurements of in-process quality.) As soon as revised production planning procedures are in place—so that the manufacturing schedule will be accurate and doable—an old measurement of schedule adherence will be reinstituted.

Maintaining a certain level of product quality—conformance to customer specs—is part of JKL's target market position but is not covered in the action plan. Quality levels already meet or exceed customer benchmarks, and working to raise those levels further is standard procedure. Quality was and is measured in-process at each operation and rigorously adhered to: no defective product is shipped, and minor exception conditions that are acceptable to customers are recorded and reported to them. The proportion of product shipped without exception conditions is a new measurement. This focuses attention on *shipped* (as distinct from in-process) quality, which is the customer viewpoint. Quality control's inspection role is now limited to finished goods, from which it compiles the new measurement of quality as shipped.

Since in-process quality determines shipped quality, and schedule adherence determines delivery performance, in-process quality and schedule adherence are also measured. This provides day-to-day feedback relative to the target market position. However, measurements of in-process quality and schedule adherence are taken for tracking purposes only, not as quantitative input to the reward system. Evaluating the performance of people who measure in-process quality—shop-floor operators—would risk penalizing them for factors outside their control (e.g., drawings, materials, equipment maintenance). And evaluating operators' performance on the basis of schedule adherence would risk sacrificing quality for expedience. As management of JKL sees it, when operators are responsible for taking their own quality measurements—measuring the results of their own work—doing so accurately is a matter of integrity. Insisting on schedule adherence would violate that integrity.

Internal operational measurements at JKL are safety (an old measurement) and productivity (redefined), in that order. Safety comes first because people matter more than machines. Productivity is defined in terms of machine time spent on *good* product. These measurements are taken for tracking purposes only—though an extended period with a good safety record is a cause for rejoicing and congratulations.

All the above measurements are compiled weekly and the charts are posted on bulletin boards. Charts show actual measurements and target levels.

The primary *financial measurement* at JKL is operating profit. Measurement of profit drivers is secondary and is used for tracking purposes only. Key profitability drivers in addition to revenue are also under the JKL division's control. These are the cost of ensuring high delivered quality, which is based on the value of rework or scrap and on the number of inspectors in quality control; and the cost of data-processing support allocated in from another business unit from which JKL was to wean itself. Leaving these costs on the other unit's books while this weaning is effected would have masked the division's true profitability.

Targeted operating profit is the primary input to the reward system for JKL's management team and replaces sales revenue as the figure looked at first by corporate executives. A shortfall from projected revenue is irrelevant if the profit plan is met. But achieving the profit plan at the expense of action plan milestones and operational measurements is not acceptable: It amounts to mortgaging the future.

As before, financial measurements are reviewed formally each month. Return on total capital invested is determined annually, along with estimates of market share, defined as share of demand in a certain customer segment.

Which measurements you deem need adjusting in what way, how they are to be used, and which carry the greatest weight depend entirely on your company's situation and goals. However, whatever the specific adjustments, having and emphasizing measurements indicating companywide performance will encourage concerted action oriented to customers and bottom-line results. Such measurements will also ensure that you receive the key, quantitative information needed for tracking purposes and for input to the reward system. And when implementation is far enough along to show up in operational measurements, that information will provide concrete evidence of progress toward target levels of performance for customers.

Revising the Reward System to Highlight Results

An inappropriate reward system does more to undermine delivery of value for customers—and, consequently, profits for the company—than any other aspect of the organizational infrastructure. Rewards are usually viewed from the company's perspective and in financial terms, that is, as "total comp" and its components: pay scales or salary levels, incentives such as bonuses, and benefits. But to people on the receiving end, the reward system is broader, encompassing all forms of reward that higher-ups can bestow on behalf of the company. The words and deeds of bosses at all levels—pats on the back, public recognition, tangible tokens of appreciation, greater responsibility—are all part of the perceived reward system. These have meaning that "total comp" lacks.

Employees give up certain rights (freedom of movement, claim to the fruits of their efforts) for which they are compensated. The strongest signal compensation can send is therefore negative: fear of loss of financial security. Positive, and more informative, is reward for meritorious performance: achievement of certain results, outstanding execution of certain duties, and display of certain conduct, such as courage and integrity. To be fully effective, a reward system does more than compensate—it sends signals that guide effort, brainpower, and behavior.

Rewards are a touchy and complex subject and tend to remain unchanged. Any adjustment to emphasize performance for customers has to take other factors into consideration too. What is to be rewarded, and how? As beauty is in the eye of the beholder, so reward is in the eye of the recipient.

Many companies and people evidently still believe that reward beyond compensation is unwarranted, seeking no more of a person than they would of a piece of equipment: routine, unexceptional effort without thought, concern, imagination, or perseverance. A reward system based on this philosophy discourages people from making a contribution and wastes the company's most important asset.

Since companies essentially have access to the same equipment and technology, it is how these are used to produce value for customers and profits for the company that makes the difference between success and failure. That difference is in the hands of people throughout the organization. Treating people at all levels with dignity and as human beings who can make a contribution releases, channels, and reinforces their inner motivation. These days, allegiance to an organization can no longer be assumed; it does, however, tend to attach to whatever one has made a personal investment in.

Signs of Appreciation. Most people are willing to do more than just put their time into their jobs; they want to do them well, know when they have done so, and derive satisfaction from it. Nonetheless, even the most self-motivated people need to know from time to time that their efforts are acknowledged and sanctioned and to feel that their achievements are appreciated. The right kind of attention is powerful at all levels, not just at lower levels.

Fortunately, nonmonetary rewards are effective and inexpensive, since the funding for pay increases can be in tight supply. And as organizational structures flatten, there are fewer opportunities for promotion. The great value of symbolic reward is that it can convey approval and appreciation as effectively as higher pay and promotions. A brief word of praise can make even hardened skeptics glow with pride, revitalizing their willingness to strive.

Most people these days don't expect extravagant rewards—only appreciation when it's due. Yet in many organizations, *any* feedback is unusual, and what there is tends to be negative. Attention, often blaming or belittling, usually gets paid only when something goes wrong. A shortfall (the lost order, the late production batch) gets intense attention while achievement (orders obtained, batches completed in the face of innumerable difficulties) goes unnoticed. Positive feedback is, therefore, rare. But positive feedback is extraordinarily effective, especially when it comes from people from levels above an immediate supervisor.

People throughout the organization watch for and interpret why, when, and how rewards are given or withheld to learn what those in authority think is important. The clearer the connection between performance and reward, the less the need for people to try to figure out whether and how performance and reward are connected. Obscure connections mean that a powerful opportunity to guide action, build morale, and nourish team spirit has been squandered.

There's no such thing as a perfect reward system. Some complaints of inequity are inevitable; handling them is part of any supervisory job. When evaluating performance, use of judgment is unavoidable; performance cannot be measured precisely. Nor can the subject of rewards be disposed of through formal procedures as if merely an administrative matter. A formal program, such as management by objectives, can be only as effective as the objectives it embodies, the fairness and judgment of the people who conduct reviews, their knowledge of the work being done, and the suitability of rewards flowing (or not) to meritorious (or otherwise) performance. Such a program is no substitute for timely in-person attention, feedback, and support. Moreover, the objectives in such programs tend to focus on a particular function or department rather than the company or business unit as a whole.

Seeing What to Adjust. When examining where the current reward system needs adjusting, you have to be ruthlessly critical of it, from the viewpoint of those whose performance is to be rewarded (or not). Particular problems might have been flagged during the course of Step Two, but people are usually reluctant to bring such things to light, meaning that you have some delving and, possibly, some soul-searching to do. You have to consider how the current system actually works and whether the perceived signals prompt productive and proper action. Figure 3-11 lists some common situations and the inappropriate—even absurd—messages they convey.

Even if the current system is flawed, it probably doesn't need a total overhaul. Certain conventions about rewards are accepted. Customary rewards for people in sales include handsome certificates, watches with the company insignia, special mention at company gatherings, and company-paid trips with spouses to exotic locations. Most people know that selling is tough and don't begrudge the extras that salespeople receive. Similarly, it's understood that people in marketing go to good restaurants at company expense, technical specialists have their work published, people who travel accumulate airline mileage for personal use, and people in the front office and at higher levels work in attractive surroundings. Yet such perks and trappings rarely come the way of most of the people whose work produces value for customers.

Inadequate consideration of customer-related work is a common flaw in reward systems. Such work is mainly nuts-and-bolts shirtsleeves stuff. Making products, preparing shipments, managing accounts receivable, and solving customers' problems lack the glamor of creating marketing programs and attending meetings on new product concepts. Moreover, customer-related work is done in lowly surroundings—in the salesperson's car, at a lab bench, from a telephone in the warehouse, on the factory floor, and on the loading dock.

Finding ways to convey the significance of, and demonstrate appreciation for, the efforts of people who contribute directly to delivering value to customers is vital. Especially in large established organizations, imagination is called for. Corporate policy often limits variation among business units and locations, but the options are many: a photograph on the wall in the reception area; a

Figure 3-11. Reward system messages.

Circumstance	Implication	Interpretation	Constructive Messages
A certain function or department is "king" and automatically gets the lion's share of the spoils.	Contributions of other parts of the company are less significant.	If you're not in *the* department, what you do doesn't count for much; if this bothers you, you put in for a transfer.	The interests of the organization as a whole take precedence over those of its parts.
Promotions go to people who make themselves look good (dig holes in good successors, go by the book at all times, are smooth talkers).	An ounce of appearance is worth a pound of performance; personal goals take precedence over the company's interests.	Self-promoting games are acceptable and even expected; if they go wrong, you make excuses or put the blame elsewhere.	Serving customers has top priority. *Everybody* is expected to pull their weight.
Managers shrug at ideas and suggestions, condemn the bearer of bad news, or criticize people in front of others.	Maintaining the status quo is more important than taking the initiative, being honest, and having the courage to step forward.	I'm not meant to think or use my judgment and conscience, but to follow marching orders to the letter—regardless.	Outstanding effort and performance are acknowledged and worthwhile. Performance is the first consideration in distribution of rewards.
A higher-up's favorite gets special treatment (plum assignments and rewards, a nicer office).	Relationships matter more than on-the-job performance.	The way you get ahead—or whatever else you want—is to pick a higher-up and please him or her.	Promotion is based mainly on the person's ability to do the job.
Stock options are available to higher-level employees only; only they have access to company results and plans; there are gross inequities in pay increases and bonuses at different levels.	Only senior people are interested in company performance, their work is by far the most important, and only their loyalty matters.	We at lower levels are just another resource, expendable and uncaring; our work doesn't matter much; we're considered untrustworthy or too stupid to understand.	Politicking and playing games are a waste of time and money and are frowned on. The knowledge, skills, ideas, and efforts of people at lower levels are valuable and appreciated.
Bonuses are the same for outstanding and so-so performers alike.	Mediocre performance is acceptable; outstanding performance goes unnoticed.	Whether you make an effort and do your job well is purely a matter of each individual's choice.	Occasional and innocent mistakes are forgiven.
Bigger titles go to people who enlarge their departments, operate as soloists, make unreasonable demands, abuse privilege, make repeated mistakes, or take part in or condone wrongdoing.	Inefficiency and poor leadership are rewarded and incompetence tolerated; lip service—to teamwork, people as the most valuable asset, participation, ethics, the good of the company and the community—is enough.	There's little reason *not* to do whatever you want, however you want, and to take what you can get.	Consistently poor performance and conscious wrongdoing are not tolerated. The earlier that problems are attended to the better, and there's no need to fear bringing them to light.

write-up in the company newsletter; time off with pay; a portion of cash savings realized through implemented suggestions. Asking employees what constitutes a reward can produce other ideas: a laudatory memo in the person's file with a copy to his or her supervisor, or a once-in-a-lifetime trip to headquarters after countless telephone conversations with people who work there.

Taking trouble to ensure that the reward system recognizes accomplishments and extra effort in all functions and at all levels is not a matter of fairness, sentiment, or altruism. Generous rewards and recognition for the people whose efforts add up to value for customers make hard-nosed business sense. An entire company that is fired up about serving customers is close to unbeatable.

Emphasis on Results. This customer orientation must be reflected in the reward system. Work to maintain or advance performance for customers as outlined in the action plan warrants greater reward than improvement in an area of minimal significance to customers or profits. The emphasis should be on attaining targets rather than gaining on past performance. This focuses efforts and resources on what the company is aiming to achieve and provides a unified sense of purpose. Group efforts focused on the company's goals are more important than individual task-oriented efforts.

This broad, results-oriented scope underscores the fact that people throughout the organization—in all functions and at all levels—contribute to its performance for customers and financially. Such scope also avoids the situation in which narrowly defined entities—a plant, a district sales office, a distribution location, a certain department—are rewarded for outstanding performance when the company as a whole turned in poor bottom-line results. The priorities and performance of the company as a whole *must* come before those of its constituent parts. Emphasizing companywide performance also takes advantage of peer pressure and concern about being the weak link. This encourages people to strive together for the greater good rather than take an it's-not-my-job attitude.

You might also need to use the reward system to encourage certain attitudes and behaviors: collaboration, dependability, integrity, initiative.

How and When to Reward. *What* constitutes a reward depends largely on people's preferences. To some people, power, glory, and money matter most; others see more obligation than privilege in greater responsibility and would prefer to learn new skills or work on more challenging assignments. Some people are uncomfortable in the spotlight, preferring to be part of a group rather than singled out.

Company styles differ too. Some companies distribute cash rewards, and others use hoopla (plaques, awards, applause) or contests. Other companies are more formal, using, for example, a congratulatory memo from a senior manager.

Tying the type of reward to what's being rewarded makes the connection between the two clear. Such tie-ins include paying for meals when people work overtime or giving time off with pay after a spell of exceptionally long days. Another way of connecting performance and reward is by recognizing a significant achievement or extra effort promptly.

The people closest to the work are in the best position to determine when outstanding performance occurs. Some companies give even the lowest-level supervisors discretion over distribution of rewards. At one company, shop-floor supervisors write a one-sentence note to the division head to recommend an individual for "dinner for two." The president then sends the employee a signed invitation with a list of restaurants that accept it as authorization. The restaurant bills the company directly.

High-level recognition carries the greatest weight. The CEO at one company recognizes achievements personally and immediately with visits or, for remote locations, telephone calls.

A fair reward system is not one that rewards equally but one that recognizes out-of-the-ordinary performance and behavior, whether good and bad. Inaction in the face of unacceptable performance is not a kindness but a cop-out. Allowing the unacceptable behavior to continue is fair to neither the individual nor the rest of the company.

Penalties for violating legal requirements and other aspects of the company's code of ethics are usually clearly defined. More complex is handling poor performance. Again, this is largely a matter of the company's norms in certain situations. Stipulating that substandard performance *will* be acted on is more important than defining the possible outcomes if poor performance continues. Being taken off an important project, being given diminished responsibility, and being demoted are among the options. The appropriate penalty can be decided at the time, based on the circumstances.

Discussion between the principals and documentation of incidents of unacceptable performance shortly after they occur can be enough to prevent recurrence. But if not, further action is essential. Tolerating someone's repeated mistakes, failures to meet deadlines, or other frowned-on behavior will send the wrong signals to everyone in the organization. It also undermines the effects of positive rewards. Without penalties, reward loses its value.

Making adjustments to your current reward system ensures that it reinforces the new direction, overall priorities, and achievement of performance targets for customers and the bottom line. A good reward system encourages productive and appropriate action and allows managers at all levels to demonstrate that they are aware of and appreciate individual and group efforts.

▲   ▲   ▲

Review of the organizational infrastructure is now complete, setting the stage for successful implementation. Necessary adjustments have been identified to make all aspects of the infrastructure consistent with one another and in keeping with customer-oriented changes, a focus on serving customers in general, and achievement of bottom-line results.

The remaining task before initiating implementation is for the management team to confirm that the conclusions reached throughout this step make up a viable, complete, and cohesive whole. Final documentation can then be compiled.

Part E: Management Team Sanction

In the last part of Step Three—The Crux, you review the conclusions of the previous parts as a whole, possibly making revisions. You then complete any additional documentation. Part E is highlighted in Figure 3-12.

Figure 3-12. Step Three—The Crux: Establishing the New Direction, Part E.

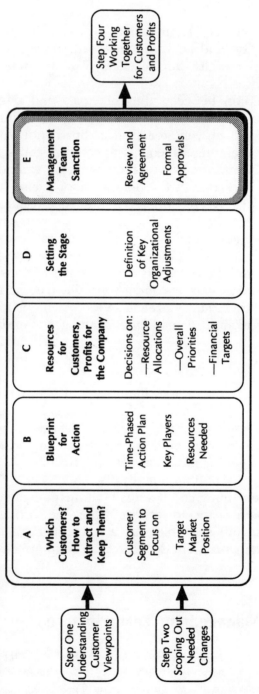

▲   ▲   ▲

When setting direction in terms of customers, especially for the first time, defining organizational adjustments is likely to take you far afield and into some detail. At this point, it's wise to take an overall look at the conclusions reached throughout this step to be sure that they add up to a complete and cohesive whole that's doable. Lingering doubts can undermine the conviction needed to get customer-oriented changes off to a good start and keep them on track.

Considering the conclusions as a whole ensures that no gaps or incongruities remain that will turn up as stumbling blocks later when implementation is under way. Reviewing the written versions of all aspects of the new direction serves to validate them. Omissions and discrepancies not apparent when arriving at individual decisions can leap from the page when they are reviewed as a whole.

Another crucial consideration is that the wording be as clear and simple as possible. Any difficulty in understanding it now will be magnified later when trying to communicate to people lower down in the organization what the company is setting out to achieve and how.

Validating Implementation Preparations

Consistency among the conclusions reached throughout this step is the primary consideration, starting with direction defined in customers' terms. This direction provides the theme to be echoed in subsequent decisions. Validation of the new direction and the decisions that flow from it is based on the facts, logic, and good judgment. What's needed is a balance between excitement about new possibilities (which tends to produce excess optimism) and fear of the unknown (which tends to produce conservatism).

Reviewing sequentially the conclusions of the first four parts of Step Three—The Crux serves to confirm the validity of each conclusion and their overall consistency. Some validating questions for each part follow.

Part A: Which Customers? How to Attract and Keep Them?

▲ Why does a particular customer segment warrant further resource commitment whereas another does not?

▲ Do all major resource commitments target a customer segment or segments where the profit potential offers at least adequate investment returns?

▲ Why is a particular customer value element emphasized in one customer segment while a different element is emphasized in another?

Part B: Blueprint for Action

▲ Considering the specific actions needed, can we really realize the performance targeted within the time indicated?

▲ Why was a particular approach to accomplish a needed change believed to be more workable and cost-effective than others?

▲ Are the stated resource requirements really adequate?

▲ Do the people identified to take a leading role in implementation feel ready and willing to do so?

Part C: Resources for Customers, Profits for the Company

▲ Are customer-related topics sufficiently high on the priority list?

▲ Are the priorities stated as simply and clearly as possible?

▲ Could the focus on key priorities be tightened even further to free resources and lift projected results?

▲ Do resource allocations reflect a proper balance between serving customers and attending to topics of internal significance and between the short and long term?

▲ Are the targeted results adequately—but not overly—ambitious?

Part D: Setting the Stage

▲ Will organizational adjustments send clear and consistent messages about what is and is not considered productive action and appropriate conduct?

▲ Do any organizational adjustments affect action plan timing and, therefore, the financial results targeted?
▲ As you look at resource reallocations and organizational adjustments from the perspective of people at lower levels, are there inconsistencies or inequities? Are these warranted?

Some final broad questions are less concrete but vital. These have to do with the management team members' views and roles:

▲ Is the amount of newness and the pace appropriate for the company? Is the work load realistically distributed among management team members?
▲ Can each management team member, and the management team as a whole, buy in to the changes—even if they have to do things differently themselves?

Once all members of the management team are satisfied that the conclusions make up a workable whole that's the best it can be, documents prepared in each of the previous parts of Step Three—The Crux can be revised, if necessary.

Preparing Additional Documentation

Documents describing the new direction need to be kept at hand. These will be used shortly for communications purposes when initiating implementation and for reference when it's under way.

Should you be seeking additional resources—whether in staffing or capital—the requisite documentation to support the increase at your company can be compiled by drawing on the conclusions of all three steps. These make a compelling case, delineating the real need for and concrete benefits of resource additions.

Additional paperwork might also be for strategic plan documentation. Information on the future market; on customers' views, needs, and objectives; and on competitors' current and probable capabilities and actions can be an eye-opener for people reviewing and approving the strategic plan.

A division of a company providing products and services to government agencies used back-up information in this way. About that time, corporate management was considering overhauling the strategic planning system. The division's management team was therefore somewhat surprised that its plan was promptly approved as written. This plan called for substantial resource additions to capitalize on market opportunities and company strengths that no one at the division or corporate level had been fully aware of. Moreover, the way the plan was documented and presented was dubbed "exemplary" by corporate management and board members. They asked the division's management team members to explain to other divisions how they had come up with their plan.

▲   ▲   ▲

You now have the solution to the business issue you set out to address, and you have made preparations for implementation to go smoothly and expeditiously. Concerted action to put the solution into practice—and thus realize improved financial results—is the subject of the last step in the CORe Method.

Recap of Step Three—The Crux

In Step Three, you defined direction in terms of customers by using information about the market, customers, and competitors (developed in Step One—The Context: Understanding Customer Viewpoints) and information about the changes needed internally and the time and resources involved (developed in Step Two—Concreteness: Scoping Out Needed Changes). On the basis of this direction, you made preparations to pursue it successfully, thus removing the usual stumbling blocks to smooth and effective implementation.

In particular, the active participation of all management team members allowed each one to build his or her confidence in the new direction, the preparations made, and the attainability of financial targets. This broad and strong endorsement at the top will be evident to the rest of the company or business unit and contribute directly to implementation success.

Figure 3-13 shows what was done in Step Three.

Figure 3-13. Step Three—The Crux: Establishing the New Direction, recap.

Part	What You Achieved and How
A Which Customers? How to Attract and Keep Them?	Determined the company's target position in an important customer segment and thereby uncovered the product or service attributes whose improvement will have the greatest impact on value for customers and financial results by: ▲ Ascertaining customer segment potential for profits and returns in light of customer prospects and viewpoints, the competitive situation, and implementation requirements ▲ Stipulating the customer-value elements to emphasize to provide value for customers, build on the company's current strengths, and match or beat competitors
B Blueprint for Action	Developed a plan of action to guide implementation in all parts of the organization by: ▲ Laying out a comprehensive time-phased action plan and compressing the timing wherever possible ▲ Summarizing resource types according to when they are needed, including the key people and any resource additions for new capabilities
C Resources for Customers, Profits for the Company	Decided on resource allocations and overall priorities in light of the new direction and agreed on the best possible financial targets by: ▲ Reallocating existing resources to customer-oriented changes and other key topics ▲ Specifying current activities and projects that will have low priority or be abandoned ▲ Projecting financial outcomes and refining resource allocations as necessary to ascertain the best outcomes realistically attainable, and revising action plan timing accordingly
D Setting the Stage	Defined how to remove organizational hurdles to smooth and effective implementation by: ▲ Reviewing and revising as needed roles and responsibilities, the organizational structure, business performance measurements, and the reward system
E Management Team Sanction	Solidified commitment to lead concerted action and realize targeted results and prepared to communicate the new direction to the people who will act on it by: ▲ Ensuring that the definition of the new direction and the preparations to pursue it are cohesive and consistent ▲ Reviewing the written version of the new direction and related decisions for clarity and brevity ▲ Preparing any formal documentation needed to obtain approvals

Step Four

The Culmination: Working Together for Customers and Profits

In Steps One and Two, you produce information to use in Step Three, where you decide on direction and financial targets and prepare for implementation. In Step Four, you set in motion and lead implementation activities throughout the company or business unit that result in superior value for customers and higher profits for the company. Action plan implementation, day-to-day activities, and ongoing improvement projects proceed in concert, unified by orientation to customers and bottom-line results. As action plan milestones are passed, performance for customers approaches target levels. Serving current customers more effectively, attracting and serving new customers, and making more productive use of all resources lifts financial results to target levels. Replanning as needed sustains the effect.

▲   ▲   ▲

Step Four has four parts:

Part A Customers—The Common Cause
Part B Self-Managed Teams
Part C Concerted Action for Rapid Progress
Part D Bottom-Line Benefits

An overview of Step Four is shown in Figure 4-1.

Figure 4-1. Step Four—The Culmination: Working Together for Customers and Profits.

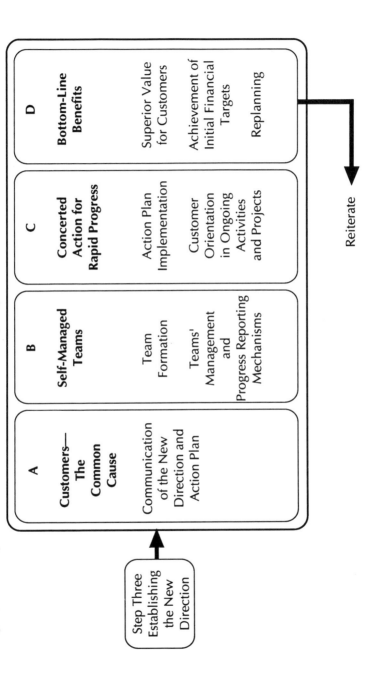

A

Customers— The Common Cause

Communication of the New Direction and Action Plan

B

Self-Managed Teams

Team Formation

Teams' Management and Progress Reporting Mechanisms

C

Concerted Action for Rapid Progress

Action Plan Implementation

Customer Orientation in Ongoing Activities and Projects

D

Bottom-Line Benefits

Superior Value for Customers

Achievement of Initial Financial Targets

Replanning

Step Three Establishing the New Direction

Reiterate

It is here that you realize results for customers and for the company—now and for the future—by resolving the business issue you set out to address. Such results include:

▲ Delivery of products and services that meet customers' needs
▲ Preferred supplier status attained or sustained through response to changes in customers' priorities and needs
▲ Competitive encroachment fended off or a loss of business reversed by positive, nonprice differentiation of significance to customers
▲ More effective interactions among departments as attention focuses on customers
▲ Market opportunities being capitalized on with limited new investment to raise both profitability and returns
▲ Pursuit of growth initiatives for the future *and* continuation of a high level of service to current customers
▲ Financial benefits materializing from formerly floundering or disappointing improvement efforts
▲ More successful development and introduction of new and revised products and services
▲ More productive use of existing resources through tighter focus on current market areas with attractive profit potential
▲ Above-average financial performance from highly selective investment of capital

Common managerial situations are also addressed in Step Four. These include:

▲ Time and energies being focused on matters of little significance to customers or the company's results
▲ People whose work affects customers having sketchy knowledge about who the key customers are and what they are looking for
▲ Low awareness of how everyday activities and teamwork affect company performance
▲ Excessive time and resources spend on administering and coordinating multiple projects
▲ Loss of talented people to competitors

▲ Poor understanding of the company's aims and priorities
▲ People going through the motions but emotionally disengaged
▲ Confusion about what constitutes outstanding or poor performance
▲ Inadequate information on project status
▲ Resistance to change based on fear of the unknown
▲ Short-term make-the-numbers maneuvers that detract from delivery of value to customers
▲ Market developments that aren't known about or market information that doesn't reach the people who need it

The Key to Improved Results: Hands-On Leadership

Having reached Step Four, you've planned more rigorously than most companies ever do and given yourself the tools to guide action and monitor progress. But no matter how thoroughly you've planned and prepared, the ultimate test of effective planning is achievement of targeted results.

Giving the go-ahead and handing off responsibility for implementation doesn't work. Yet in many companies, this is precisely what happens: Once a plan or new program has been approved by management, implementation gets the attention afforded an afterthought, as though the existence of a plan is the end of the process. Should implementation get started, it usually founders.

The consequence is the same when implementation is launched with a fanfare (rousing speeches, banners, and posters), and management turns its attention to other matters. A vicious cycle ensues: Early enthusiasm disintegrates into excuses, finger pointing, and detachment from an effort that cannot succeed, causing more excuses, and so on. In the worst case, business as usual prevails, and drastic measures are then needed to bring actual results in line with short-term targets.

Keeping implementation on course to produce targeted results isn't easy. The toughest job for any business unit management team—especially the general manager—is to get the organization moving and operating as a cohesive whole. The driving and unifying force is that team's leadership.

Management's active involvement makes it clear to everyone else that accomplishing changes to serve customers more effectively is the key to greater prosperity for the company in the near term and beyond. People pick up on that evident resolve and respond accordingly: Self-interest encourages them to do so. The need for last-minute maneuvers and heavy-handedness is reduced.

Such leadership will allow everyone—from the executive suite to the shop floor—to enjoy and share in a sense of accomplishment for a job well done and the rewards that flow from achievement of financial targets. Moreover, the experience of success breeds confidence to face and master what the future brings.

Part A: Customers—The Common Cause

You introduce the new direction—the target market position, the action plan to attain it, restated overall priorities, resource reallocations, and any organizational adjustments that are to take effect in the short-term—to the people who will be guided by it. Part A is highlighted in Figure 4-2.

▲   ▲   ▲

The outcomes of management team deliberations are always news to the rest of the organization. The fact that you've given the action plan the go-ahead has to be made known. The people in various functions and at different levels who contributed in Step Two and whose views were sought during action plan development are expecting to hear the outcome of your deliberations. These people will be curious about what became of their efforts and recommendations.

Informing people that action to improve performance for customers is now to begin, however, is only one consideration. Equally important is communicating how the new direction affects day-to-day activities and other projects so implementation isn't seen as a separate endeavor.

Figure 4-2. Step Four—The Culmination: Working Together for Customers and Profits, Part A.

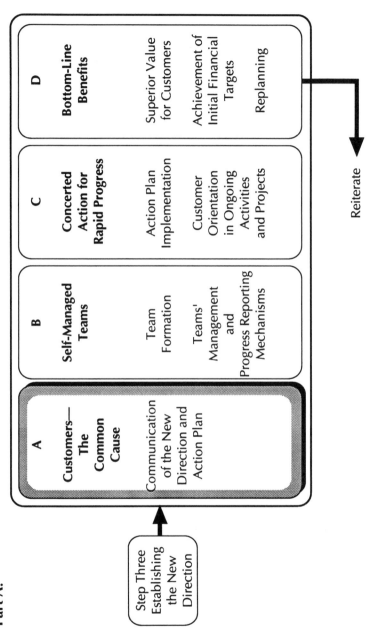

Conveying Useful, Interesting Information

Specifying how much is to be communicated how soon lets you control proprietary or sensitive information while providing the details needed to foster support for implementation and to guide everyday decisions and actions at lower levels. Once action is under way, what is being worked on will become common knowledge anyway. If people don't have a clear understanding of why the action is being taken—the reasoning behind it and what it's intended to achieve—the apparent secrecy and resulting speculation can hinder progress.

Fortunately, the information you're most likely not to want to disclose is probably the least interesting to people at lower levels, such as the company's financial targets and long-term possibilities. At a company making precision metal components, communication of its plan omitted profit targets, undecided details about changes in the reward system, longer-term hiring plans, and the possibilities of eventually entering a new market segment and of acquiring another company. The omissions went unnoticed.

People are usually most interested in what they can relate to, that is, what affects their work. Thus, the information of greatest interest is also that which is most useful for people throughout the company to know. This includes customers' views of the company and its competitors and competitors' actions and their significance. When reviewing information such as that in Figure 4-3 with people at lower levels, management members should make evident their conviction that performance targets are attainable and their understanding that these will not be achieved overnight.

If this is the first time such information is shared, it may be necessary to set explicit ground rules about confidentiality. Being privy to this information carries an obligation: Honor management's trust. The ground rules are for the management team to decide; for example, information about customers, competitors, and the company's plans should not be passed on, orally or in writing, to outsiders without specific agreement from a superior in advance.

Getting the Message Across Effectively

Using everyday channels to spread the word avoids the drawbacks of formal employee communication sessions. The cer-

Figure 4-3. Information on customer-oriented company plans.

Customer Value Element	Theme	Impact	
		Continue as Is	*Customer-Oriented Change*
Product	Maintain and improve	Meet customer specifications for delivered quality and minimize acceptable exception conditions	
Transaction	Advance		Reduce turnaround time on first shipment by 50%; then deliver according to latest customer schedule; provide complete production records with shipment
Pricing	External: maintain	Current pricing policy (short term)	
	Internal: improve		Reduce cost of supplying quality product on time by 20% (long term)
Support	Maintain and advance	Provide current presale and postsale assistance	Provide compilation of quality and delivery performance for customers' supplier evaluation

emonial nature of such presentations—especially when out-of-the-ordinary—means that experienced people tend to view what they hear with suspicion or skepticism. Is this really an early, sanitized sign that a bad-news event—restructuring or sale of the business unit—is in the works? Is this just another flavor-of-the-month program, more lip service about teamwork and people being the most valuable assets, and more flag waving about the need to do more with less?

The inherent formality of large sessions generally makes them ineffectual: Information flows only one way. The effect of plans and new initiatives on day-to-day realities is rarely addressed, and questions on this point are limited. The attendants at such sessions therefore return to their workplaces little the wiser about whether and how they are supposed to do their jobs differently.

Recognizing the inadequacies of large sessions for communication purposes, the president of one company established an additional forum. During the course of a year, every person in the division attends a meeting of ten to fifteen people from different functions and levels at which the president shares current information about the business and answers any related questions. Only personal topics are disallowed. If the president doesn't know the answer, he says so and makes sure that he finds out and relays the information within a few days. Occasionally, maintaining confidentiality about corporate plans means that he can't give a full answer. If this is the case, he says so; this explanation is accepted. These informal get-togethers are expected to continue indefinitely, augmenting existing communication forums.

You might have regularly scheduled forums that are suitable for communicating the company's direction, such as weekly staff meetings or small group sessions at quarterly sales meetings. Small forums allow you to present information in a way that's tailored to the participants and encourage their questions and discussion so that they can understand how company plans affect current activities and priorities.

Having middle managers relay to the people who report to them what they've heard from management team members indicates that, rather than being circumvented and their roles undermined, they have an important part to play in moving the company forward. Having a senior manager attend sessions conducted by middle managers avoids putting them in an uncomfortable position: having to get across (clearly and convincingly) new information to the people who report to them. Middle managers may have recommendations about how best to relay the information, such as in a joint session with a colleague so that people from two areas who customarily work together hear the same thing at the same time. At a parts manufacturer, a manager had the idea of borrowing a fully assembled product from a customer so that people who work on the components could see what becomes of them and why certain characteristics are so important.

Ensuring Listeners' Understanding

What's communicated will be easily and quickly understood if it's explained briefly and simply. Explanations of how conclusions were arrived at in Step Three—The Crux: Establishing the New Direction are unnecessary. The basic facts and logic behind the conclusions are straightforward, can be described in simple terms. For example:

▲ Demand from a certain customer segment isn't growing as it used to since government programs are being cut back.
▲ Increased competition and price cuts have reduced margins to the point where the company needs to expand into other areas to make money in the future.
▲ The company's strengths fit better in some market areas than in others.

Questions and concerns are almost certain to arise. This is less to challenge what's being heard than to confirm understanding. For example, in light of action to increase forecast accuracy and advance delivery performance, what's going to happen with the project to adopt a new production planning methodology? Will the project be abandoned entirely? Reinstituted later? You already have the answers to such questions: You determined them when deciding on resource allocations and overall priorities.

Other questions are likely to address factors on which the action plan is based. For example:

▲ Where did the idea come from that someone in order processing is now to issue certain orders to manufacturing, instead of marketing issuing the authorization as in the past? Does marketing know of this change? You can explain that the action plan incorporates recommendations made by people from both order processing and marketing. Most people won't know this and may have some concern about the change making sense and the key players going along with it.

▲ How was it determined that specific product configuration changes are now crucial? Again, some people who participated in Step Two—Concreteness: Scoping Out Needed Changes will know that certain high-potential customers consider the company's products cumbersome to handle and use. You can explain to the others that these customers are streamlining their operations and, therefore, that product revisions are the key to cementing relationships with current customers and attracting new ones.

Responses to and discussions around such questions and concerns allow people to establish their own confidence in the success of the new direction. This encourages them to participate and contribute rather than hold back and wait and see or, worse, fight the new direction.

Getting Positive Reactions

Naturally, not all people will immediately like, agree with, and buy into all aspects of what they hear. Some debate, second-guessing, and critical commentary are inevitable. Some people are likely to resent the change in priorities no matter how rationally and persuasively you present them. And a few dissident voices are likely to make themselves heard. Overall, however, reactions are likely to be favorable.

Your action plan and related changes are almost certain to address topics that people already know to be problematic and systemic. The prospect of relief from old problems can make news of change good news. For example, at a company making assemblies for temperature control systems, people welcomed the action plan. Those who prepared shipments (and who had to scrounge around for parts to complete them) and those with whom customers got angry (when told that the spares they needed weren't available) were delighted to hear that demand for replacement parts was to be incorporated into production plans. Other people were relieved to see that the action plan addressed other ingrained practices such as jerry-rigging manufacturing processes to accommodate engineering change orders issued when production was already under way; making last-minute schedule changes to meet performance measurements; and being blamed for poor product quality, labor costs in excess of standards, and inadequate attention to productivity improvements. These occurrences would become a thing of the past as planned action and related changes became reality.

Managerial Benefits of Thorough Communication

The main purpose of communicating the new direction and action plan is to introduce them in a convincing and compelling way. But as people in one area seek corroboration with colleagues in another, the grapevine works to your advantage. This reinforces the meaning, explicit and otherwise, of what's been communicated. That everybody is receiving the same information can be an eye-opener. So can the fact that there's a cohesive plan of action for all functions—one game plan evidently endorsed by all members of the management team. This signifies that teamwork is to become a reality, rather than remain a concept that's talked about, espoused by a few people, or referred to by certain individuals to mean doing things *their* way.

Making sure that information about the new direction reaches all corners of an organization is time-consuming but has lasting benefits. No member of management can participate in every decision and action that takes place hour by hour, day in and day out, throughout the company. By spreading knowledge of customers and the company's plans, you are giving people at lower levels information they need to do their jobs well.

The more fully people understand the customer viewpoint and company priorities, the easier you've made it for them to spend their time and energy in the most productive way. You've also injected a fresh awareness of how what's good for customers is good for the company and, therefore, in the best interests of managers and employees alike. Moreover, you've encouraged a two-way information flow in the future, increasing the chances that key information will reach you promptly.

The communication effort is not, of course, over and done with in a single pass: It needs repeating and updating as time goes by. Even so, establishing a foundation of common understanding can free you from unwarranted involvement in operational details, such as resolving differences of opinion, smoothing ruffled feathers, firefighting when something becomes a major problem, and listening to excuses.

The time you have to spend on such matters drops significantly once people at lower levels can make informed decisions, use their judgment more effectively, and work together more constructively. This allows you to focus on vital topics that only senior management can attend to, such as making sure that no opportunity is missed to improve future results and that the most talented people receive the career development they need to become tomorrow's effective executives.

Motivating Employees

The connections among communication of information and morale and motivation are well documented and much discussed. Yet some managers withhold information deliberately as a way to exercise power, seemingly unaware of the detrimental effect on productive action.

Sharing information does more than offset this negative. It tells people that they are perceived as being capable of understanding business considerations and as concerned and trusted employees who have a contribution to make. It also means that each person has the opportunity to learn, possibly for the first time, how his or her job relates to the company's survival and prosperity. This provides a motivating sense of purpose.

People at lower levels often don't know why they're doing what they're doing. What is the point of moving manufacturing materials from one part of the plant to another? Of maintaining adequate supplies of product information sheets? Of being polite and helpful when answering the telephone? Of keeping records of product-use problems? Such activities can be boring, but knowing that your work has significance to someone else can give it meaning.

In a customer-oriented version of a much-quoted story, four craftsmen who are doing identical jobs have different views of their work: One carpenter aspires to doing the best possible job of shaping wood; another is simply earning his living; the third is participating in building a ship; but the fourth sees beyond the end product of his work—a ship for sale. To him, the ship he's working on at the time is for people who want to travel far from home, the one he worked on before was to move goods from one country to another, and the one he'll work on next is for the navy. This carpenter sees his work in terms of the people who'll sail in the ships and what their aims are.

The fourth carpenter may have been using his imagination to project beyond the end result of his work. But a vivid imagination is unnecessary when real-world information about the company's customers and their customers is available to make mundane work seem more worthwhile. Such information has immediacy and accuracy that's missing from imaginative ponderings.

Serving customers—working to help them attain their goals—can become the common cause that people throughout the company can get excited about. Working to serve real, revenue-producing customers has power that the notion of serving internal customers lacks. It's tough to get enthusiastic about "serving" people you've worked with for years, and real customers are obviously more important because they generate the company's cash flow. Thus, in emotional and rational terms, serving real customers has greater appeal and significance.

Not all people can be inspired by the idea of serving even real customers, however. But even the most earth-bound pragmatist can see the connection between serving customers, realizing company revenue, and dispensing individual paychecks. Others can be motivated by the prospect of accolades, financial gain, or a sense of satisfaction from a job well done. Some people thrill to the challenge of fixing a problem, making an innovation work, or beating the competition. In whatever terms you appeal to individual motivation, you start by emphasizing that concerted, customer-oriented action helps the company prosper.

▲   ▲   ▲

Having established broad, common understanding of the new direction and what it entails, you now form the teams responsible for putting planned action into practice.

Part B: Self-Managed Teams

You form the team or teams that will implement the action plan and hand over responsibility to them. The teams propose, for your approval, the mechanisms they'll use to manage progress and keep you informed. Part B is highlighted in Figure 4-4.

▲   ▲   ▲

In Step Three—The Crux: Establishing the New Direction, the management team decided on implementation team members and their roles. The team members themselves have had indications of their possible involvement and have some familiarity with what the action plan covers. Some of them were involved in Step Two—Concreteness: Scoping Out Needed Changes or had a hand in developing the action plan. But the people who'll be on a team must be told that their involvement is definite, whether they are to work full or part time on implementation, and who is to lead the team. Team members also need to know who they'll be working with, what is expected of them, and the available resources, such as the work space or equipment time assigned and, if applicable, the funding. Each team also needs to get itself organized.

Forming Teams That Manage Their Own Activities

When you ask a team to develop its own detailed work plan and define the mechanisms it will use to track and report progress, team members feel the responsibility they are charged with. The work plan and tracking mechanisms are each team's self-management tools. A team acts on its own work plan, follows up on individual action items, conducts its own progress reviews, keeps its own documentation, and informs its members' superiors of progress or hurdles as these arise. It also keeps other interested parties informed, eliciting their comments or support as needed. What is to be done is focused and paced by the action plan, but how a team goes about executing its tasks and living up to its responsibilities is up to its members. This allows team members to build in efficiencies by combining implementation tasks with ongoing activities wherever possible.

Figure 4-4. Step Four—The Culmination: Working Together for Customers and Profits, Part B.

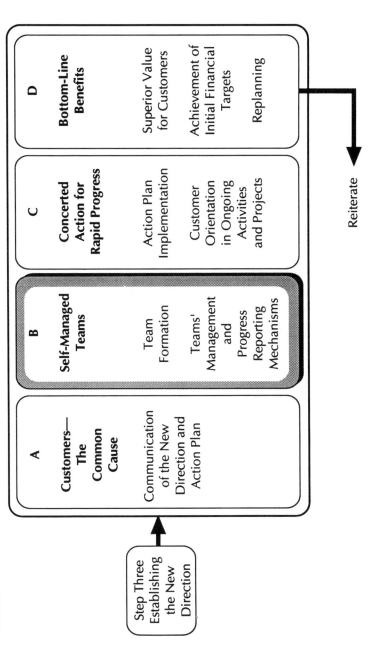

A	B	C	D
Customers— The Common Cause	**Self-Managed Teams**	**Concerted Action for Rapid Progress**	**Bottom-Line Benefits**
Communication of the New Direction and Action Plan	Team Formation	Action Plan Implementation	Superior Value for Customers
	Teams' Management and Progress Reporting Mechanisms	Customer Orientation in Ongoing Activities and Projects	Achievement of Initial Financial Targets
			Replanning

Step Three Establishing the New Direction

Reiterate

Although the new direction and planned action are likely to have been well received, some dissension about team membership can arise. People who are not part of a team might think that they should be. Some people may want to be on a different team, may not get along with other team members, or may resent not being the leader. They may also claim that they cannot work on implementation while handling their current work loads.

People can usually be persuaded to give the teams a try as set up, with the understanding that the arrangements will be changed if they don't work. And you can explain how current tasks are being reassigned to free team members' time for implementation.

Emphasize to team leaders that their responsibility includes informing you promptly of significant discord or any other causes of delay requiring your intervention. You can't support a team if you don't know when it needs help. A team's membership may need adjusting for it to function smoothly and effectively; this will become apparent as implementation moves from one stage to another.

Team members, individually and as a group, need to satisfy themselves that they fully understand the action plan and what it is intended to achieve. Ensuring this understanding is a team leader's first task; he or she can obtain clarification from you or others as needed. Only with a clear sense of the big picture will a team's work plan be properly focused and dovetail with other teams' efforts.

The composition of each team is unique. For example, at a business unit making components for aircraft, there were three teams. Two of these were headed by division management members—the vice-presidents. The division was setting out to strengthen its standing in a customer segment it had recently started doing business in. With superior performance on the Product, the principal thrust of its action plan was the Transaction. Serving customers more effectively required speeding first delivery for each order and responding to changes in dates for subsequent shipments.

For the two teams led by vice-presidents, identifying a primary and a supporting team leader (a vice-president from a different function) underscored that concerted effort was replacing past practice, when each function pursued improvements projects independently. The charter and leadership of these two teams was as follows:

▲ One team would obtain additional space and equipment and change the layout of existing equipment, led by the heads of engineering and manufacturing operations.
▲ A second team would work on having shop-floor operators become responsible for assuring in-process quality, led by the heads of manufacturing and quality control.

The third team was made up entirely of middle managers. This team's charter was to make it possible for manufacturing to produce high-quality product on time and efficiently. Initially, this charter had two parts: (1) provide computer-generated manufacturing instructions based on drawings developed on the existing computer-aided design system and (2) focus on production scheduling. Initially, current procedures would be improved by, for example, scheduling minor parts that were formerly omitted from the schedule. Then, once computer-generated manufacturing information was available, this would be incorporated into a more sophisticated scheduling system. The two parts of this effort would then merge, expanding to include other departments in the adoption and use of an integrated, computerized information system for the whole division.

This team's leader was a middle manager, the head of materials management, who reported to the head of operations. The core team was made up of people from materials management and engineering. Other team members, whose involvement would ebb and flow during implementation, included other members of materials management and engineering, shop-floor operators, and, later, other users of the new system from, for example, finance, sales, and marketing.

At this company, giving middle managers responsibility of this magnitude was a first. The aim was to establish rapport among them and to build their capabilities and confidence to take on more responsibility for day-to-day decisions. It would also reveal to division management who would be best suited for a larger role as the business grew.

At another company making consumer products that were marketed through distributors, middle-management leadership of cross-functional teams was established practice. At this company, strengthening a so-so position in a particular segment (where it had been doing business for years but in a halfhearted way) would allow profits to increase, with the growing portion of end-user demand flowing through that channel.

Achieving the target position in this customer segment called for advances on both the Product and the Transaction. The action plan included providing the same product in unbreakable containers, seeking customers' counsel on the configuration of a new product, incorporating customers' probable order quantities into production and purchasing plans, bringing order processing up to speed on customer personnel and the information needed when placing an order, and ensuring timely provision of production records for customers' quality control.

In this instance, there was one team led by a middle manager in marketing. This person, another middle manager (in sales), lower-level managers (from production planning and purchasing), and clerical people (in order processing and quality control documentation) made up the team. Other people—who would work on and off with the team but were considered members—included manufacturing managers involved in product revisions, technical people working on the new product, and someone in finance who'd assist in effecting a price increase when the time came.

Agreeing on Mechanisms to Track Progress

Mechanisms to manage and report progress are likely to vary as much as team composition. At the consumer products manufacturer mentioned above, team members were in three locations. The mechanisms they adopted applied to team members individually and the team as a whole.

The team's work plan was developed into a list for each person showing what was to be done, with whom, and by when. The core team members would hold weekly conference calls and meet periodically at the central location, setting dates to coincide with trips for other meetings. The team leader would issue a written summary of progress, and team members would also update their superiors directly. The team set itself some ground rules, such as:

▲ If a team member is not going to be able to complete an action item on time—for whatever reason—he or she will find someone else to do so or alert the team leader immediately.
▲ Any team member who would like to take a turn being the leader (chairing a progress review, following up on action items, doing the write-up) could do so.

Mechanisms designed to manage implementation may overlap with meetings and reports on other activities and projects. This can be an opportunity to streamline them. At a specialty chemicals manufacturer, the greatest overlap was with ongoing product revision efforts. There were several forums to manage these that involved essentially the same people from various departments. Each month, some fifteen people from several departments and at three levels, including senior management, met to review certain product revisions. Comprehensive minutes were issued. Fifty man-hours a month were involved in these meetings alone. New products and other types of revisions were handled separately in other forums.

Changing the way all these activities and projects were tracked would free the time of everyone involved. Some of the simplifying changes were:

▲ Combining two forums into one with broader scope to include new product introductions and all types of revisions;
▲ Revising attendance at meetings so that only the key middle managers would meet routinely; and
▲ Issuing one summary report that gave the key conclusions of the meeting and highlights of the events of the previous month. This report, and updates up the chain of command, would keep the management team informed without their attending lengthy meetings or ploughing through full meeting minutes.

New mechanisms to keep the management team abreast of implementation were not necessary for two of the teams at the aircraft component manufacturer mentioned earlier. The management team members leading the team already met frequently. However, implementation progress did become a standing item on the agenda at regularly scheduled division management meetings and at operating reviews with corporate management. The middle-management team would periodically provide written reports and in-person updates and was sometimes invited to present progress reports at the divisional staff meeting. Since the work being done by this team affected people throughout the organization, its progress would also be relayed to lower levels through regular departmental meetings.

How your teams propose to manage and report their activities and how these coincide with any established forums is, of course, impossible to predict. But having the teams describe the tracking mechanisms they'll use lets you confirm that these are defined and get an early reading on a team that might need extra guidance. It also demonstrates that you'll stay involved and ensures you receive updates directly from the people closest to what's being done—the team members themselves. Such updates are in addition to customary checkpoints, such as formal review and approval before introduction of a new product or issuance of a purchase order for new equipment.

Periodic reports on progress from the teams are only a supplement to informal day-to-day interactions in person. Giving the teams the real responsibility for realizing progress and results doesn't mean that they are being set adrift to sink or swim on their own.

▲   ▲   ▲

Once the teams are formed, have a clear understanding of what is expected of them, and have mechanisms to manage their work and keep you informed, they can forge ahead on implementation.

Part C: Concerted Action for Rapid Progress

The implementation teams get to work to accomplish the changes needed to provide superior value for customers. The teams do their best to keep progress on track, and they keep you informed and seek your guidance or intervention when necessary. You also keep an eye on how they are doing, demonstrate your interest, and provide support as needed.

At the same time, other people—those supporting implementation as well as those not involved in it—pursue day-to-day activities and other projects according to the new direction and priorities. To ensure that the teams receive the support they need, you make sure that these priorities are being adhered to and that organizational adjustments are adopted. You also convey your awareness and appreciation of signs of progress. Part C is highlighted in Figure 4-5.

▲   ▲   ▲

Even in an organization accustomed to innovation, if you or other executives turn your attention to matters other than implementation shortly after it's launched, it will almost certainly falter or go off course. If you wait until word reaches you that this has happened, it may be too late for full recovery. Your continued and evident interest makes it clear how much weight you attach to concerted customer-oriented action, implementation progress, and achievement of the new profit plan. People will respond accordingly.

Keeping Your Finger on the Pulse

No matter how sound the action plan and how broad and strong the sense of commitment, some things won't go precisely as intended. As implementation proceeds, unforeseeable events will occur. Perhaps the first-choice distributor to supply and service remote customers will have other plans. Or customers' reactions to a product revision will indicate that it hasn't hit the mark on the first try. A skilled and knowledgeable team leader can handle most such setbacks, especially in an organization accustomed to innovation and teamwork. But even such team leaders need to check that management agrees with the remedial action they propose.

Incidents that arise in the regular course of doing business are almost certain to affect implementation. When making progress on implementation conflicts with serving today's customers and realizing this month's profit plan, the experienced team leader will recognize the conflict and seek guidance on immediate priorities.

Figure 4-5. Step Four—The Culmination: Working Together for Customers and Profits, Part C.

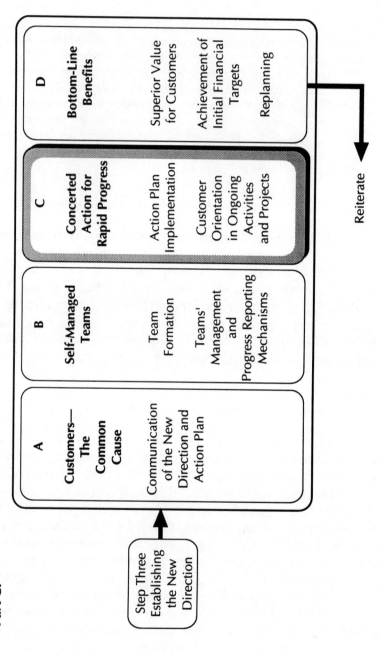

Step Three Establishing the New Direction

A

Customers— The Common Cause

Communication of the New Direction and Action Plan

B

Self-Managed Teams

Team Formation

Teams' Management and Progress Reporting Mechanisms

C

Concerted Action for Rapid Progress

Action Plan Implementation

Customer Orientation in Ongoing Activities and Projects

D

Bottom-Line Benefits

Superior Value for Customers

Achievement of Initial Financial Targets

Replanning

Reiterate

Consultation with management ensures that a clash between implementation and other activities is resolved in the most appropriate way. This attention from management also helps maintain team morale. Coming face to face with harsh realities and day-to-day imperatives can dishearten even the most enterprising and persistent people.

Some teams or team members may need a push from time to time. Good team leaders quickly find out who needs reminding to get an action item done on time, who to ask to step in when necessary, and when to urge and coax. Thus your follow-up, formal or otherwise, should start with a light touch.

Accomplishing customer-oriented changes is principally in the teams' hands. This means that maintaining their sense of ownership and responsibility is vital: The spotlight is, and must remain, on the implementation teams.

Realizing Progress

Using their self-management tools, the teams work in parallel to reach one milestone after another. How much is accomplished how early is likely to be a pleasant surprise. For example, first samples of a product revision may well be ready in record time now that people from product development, manufacturing, purchasing, and quality assurance are working together on the team—*and* the equipment time they need is made available by schedulers, *and* the people making current products need not fear being penalized for reporting lower machine utilization and higher indirect labor.

Implementation may proceed more easily than expected. At one company, early insight into future demand was essential for implementation activities and after implementation to ensure timely product supply. People on the team had thought that if they asked customers to provide information on likely volumes, customers wouldn't know what they'd need or wouldn't share this information for fear it would be misinterpreted as firm orders. The expected roadblock did not materialize. Customers promptly agreed to provide the information, then and routinely in the future.

In other instances, implementation proceeds somewhat differently from plan. At one company, a training program to add

upstream capacity for smoother manufacturing flow didn't produce the multiskilled cadre envisaged. Shop floor people were to
move around the plant as needed. However, they were reluctant to
do so because they wouldn't know in advance which area they'd be
assigned to and would be in unfamiliar surroundings with people
they wouldn't have time to get to know. But a few operators did
voice an interest in making permanent transfers. This way, they
could take full advantage of the higher pay scale in the upstream
area. The desired effect was achieved, but in a different way than
originally envisioned.

Fits and starts are likely as people adapt to change at their own
pace. At a metal-working company that was effecting long-term
cost reductions, machine operators were to assume responsibility
for in-process quality inspection and sign off. This involves much
more than rejecting a part or calling a halt to production when
something's not right. Signing a document that says the product is
right—after one has worked on it—carries a tremendous responsibility. The machine operators, being highly skilled, quickly learned
to do the inspection and complete the record. But they all held back
from what they saw as the giant step of adding their signatures,
which would stand alone, and so continued to seek someone
else's, as in the past. Then one or two operators felt ready to fly
solo. All of a sudden, others followed suit. Management's conscious decision *not* to push had been a taxing one, but it worked.

Managing the Unexpected

Having responsibility for progress, the teams are likely to do
their utmost to manage the unexpected. At one company, people
on the team and others working with them realized that the old
division of tasks no longer made sense. Rather than seek guidance
from above, the team devised a lighthearted way to disentangle the
mismatch: a list called It's Not My Job. Anyone with a task that no
longer fit with his or her work put it on the list. There was one
condition: Putting a task on the list obligated you to accept one
from it. In a matter of days a long list had appeared and disap-
peared, negotiated away by the people directly involved.

When a team recovers from the unexpected on its own, you

may not learn about it until after the fact through routine updates. Concentrating on reaching the next milestone, a team is likely to gloss over what it took to pass the preceding one. There may also be hesitance to blow the team's horn. When a feat is played down, it's up to management to recognize its value.

How a team manages the unforeseen may need your guidance or blessing. For example, when one company was installing new equipment, engineers explained that parts would be loaded and off-loaded from ladders. A suggestion arose. Building a scaffold would make machine loading quicker, avoid possible damage to the part, and be far safer. This was clearly the intelligent thing to do, but the team leader was concerned about the additional expense and unsure whether to explore or ignore the idea. The business unit president, who took regular walks around the facility, heard of the idea. Applauding it, the president asked the approximate cost and promptly suggested the team put in a work order.

Out-of-the-ordinary occurrences that happen in the regular course of doing business seem to come at the worst possible time. At a company setting out to reverse poor relationships with certain distributors, team activities were proceeding as planned when a crisis occurred. A raw material supplier had started using a new machine, but neither its tests nor the company's incoming quality control checks revealed any difference in the new machine's output. The difference became apparent only when containers of finished product were found to be opening, risking spillage and degradation of the product, since it was sensitive to light.

Efforts rallied to understand the problem and solve it. This could not happen overnight, meaning that some slippage in product supply seemed inevitable. Ironically, the thrust of implementation was dependable supply. The team members informed the customers what had happened, and their reaction was unexpectedly favorable. Already aware that the company was working to improve on-time delivery, customers listened to the measures being taken to maintain supply and asked to be kept up-to-date on the situation. A couple of distributors said that they appreciated being told of the problem; another was impressed that the company had identified the problem so early. With a sigh of relief, the team members went back to work.

It's unrealistic to expect implementation to go smoothly. But the chances are that what you lose on the curves you'll make up on the straightaway. By staying in close touch, you'll know when something unexpected occurs and be able to help the team recover and keep moving forward.

Demonstrating Your Support

Team members can usually tell when some out-of-the-ordinary and visible support from higher up is needed and may ask for it. For example, team members at a company gearing up to refurbish equipment agreed that the time had come for some internal public relations. Refurbishing used equipment differs dramatically from producing original equipment. Refurbishment involves cleaning off layers of grime instead of putting shiny new products together.

Seeing this perception as a black cloud over the next phase of implementation, the team leader hesitantly approached the plant manager and asked him to visit the team's work space on the shop floor. The team knew how important it was for the plant manager to be seen taking an interest in the project. The plant manager said yes immediately and thanked the team for letting him know how he could help. He had been holding back from paying conspicuous attention for fear of appearing to interfere or violate the chain of command.

Team members prepared a special show-and-tell demonstration to coincide with the plant manager's visit. The ripple effects were far greater than expected. His visit became the talk of the facility (at workstations, in offices, the lunchroom, the parking lot) for days, completely eclipsing the bias against refurb work for a while. The plant manager asked the team to put on a similar demonstration when corporate executives came to visit. This gave people on the team a morale boost that they hadn't known they needed.

Sometimes team leaders won't seek management support, meaning that the initiative has to be yours. How best to demonstrate continuing interest or encouragement varies with the composition of the team and your and the company's style. With team members who are professionals or in a setting that tends to formality, you or other senior managers might put an appreciative comment on a progress report, drop by the team leader's office, or ask to sit in on a team meeting. Just being there, observing, conveys that you think the team's work is important. And a favorable comment as the meeting concludes is likely to be well received. In another setting with different players, an evening beer-and-pizza party would be more suitable.

Paying Attention to Other Activities

Special attention to implementation is warranted, since it involves change that directly affects customers and company results. However, delivery of product and service attributes valued by customers, but not covered by the action plan, must be maintained. Other ongoing activities and projects must also proceed.

You may need to guard against overemphasis on action plan implementation. Association with a new, highly visible effort—especially one that's going well—can distract attention from other activities that lack novelty or that the company has less control over. Balancing attention between implementation and other matters can be tough to do.

Capitalizing on performance advances through sales and marketing activities is also crucial, but increasing current customer volumes and signing up new customers is uphill work at the best of times. At a company producing engine parts, profiting from its enhanced ability to serve customers called for establishing relationships with new customers. This required careful orchestration over a long sell cycle. Prospective customers had stated their reluctance to add suppliers. To be considered as a potential supplier meant convincing people from several divisions of a customer company. The marketing campaign was to start during implementation, anticipating its effects. Management expected the campaign to succeed slowly, but early efforts proved even less fruitful than expected. The principal reason was that senior managers concentrated on action plan implementation, paying too little attention to the marketing campaign. Realizing this, they started following up on the campaign more closely and stepped up their support. For example, the division president began going along on customer visits. This attention rejuvenated the marketing campaign.

You also have to be on the alert for the need to reinforce a customer orientation in ongoing activities and projects. Yesterday's ways won't change overnight, and slippage is likely. Occurrences such as the following need to be addressed:

▲ Customers who call in are still being put on hold, or told "it's not my department" and to call another number.
▲ Promotional programs are still highlighting points of company pride or aiming to one-up competitors.
▲ Abandoned projects are still being pursued, such as those shelved due to lack of relevance to customers or lack of cost-effectiveness.
▲ Selling efforts and product supply decisions are still favoring high gross-margin products rather than high operating-profit customers.

Adjustments to business performance measurements and the reward system can take hold particularly slowly. At one company, people still recorded the volume produced on each shift, despite the fact that management had done away with that measurement. This was partly from habit and partly out of curiosity. But they also took the measurement because comparing it with norms (the previous day's, the other shift's) gave forewarning of a possible challenge about a shortfall. Managers taking or discussing an old measurement may simply need to be reminded that it's no longer needed and that taking or talking about it sends the wrong signal.

Mid- and lower-level managers with first-time discretion over rewards may be unsure how to use it. At one company, a continuous improvement effort was yielding significant efficiencies. The manager shepherding this effort wanted to do something by way of recognition but wasn't sure what would be appropriate. Discussion with a superior produced the idea of taking a photograph of everybody involved that would appear in the company newsletter and having prints made for them to take home.

Everyday observations and discussions indicate when you need to foster orientation to customers, teamwork among parts of the organization, and recognition of accomplishment or outstanding effort. Prompt reinforcement works best. Informal interactions also provide good news: evidence of progress.

Seeing Signs of Progress

Day-to-day impressions are one way to detect positive change. The amount of time you have to spend resolving others' differences and firefighting is likely to drop. An executive at one company has estimated the time his department spends productively had doubled as a result of the new emphasis on business priorities in all departments. And when problems do arise, solutions are more quickly found and put into practice. At the company that produces engine parts, on the day operational measurements (showing delivered quality and timing of shipments) are posted, people from all functions stop by to see them. Occasionally there's a shortfall from target. A group quickly forms. Who's going to investigate? When will those investigating report what they've found? Broad, constructive interest in what's posted is to be expected because everybody's rewards are affected by it. In the past the reaction to bad news had been lengthy heated debates and finger pointing about who was to blame. However, such negative responses have been replaced by urgent attention to taking action to avoid a recurrence.

Qualitative impressions relative to the past are telling, but more significant are concrete signs of progress related to what the company is setting out to achieve. A few indicators provide evidence of action on all fronts. These indicators encompass implementation, day-to-day activities, and ongoing improvement projects throughout the company or business unit. How these few indicators relate to overall priorities is shown in Figure 4-6. (Key indicators of implementation progress are in capital letters.) Tangible indicators carry greater weight, since they are directly related to results and measurable and are therefore less subjective than intangible indicators.

What specific activities fall within a priority set at any particular time varies from company to company. The activities that have first, second, or third priority at your company were determined in Part C of Step Three—The Crux: Establishing the New Direction.

With implementation still under way, it's probably too soon for favorable comments from customers or for the company's reputation to glow more brightly. Not until the changes being made during implementation are in place will results be noticeable

Figure 4-6. Indicators of progress.

Priority/Key Beneficiary	Activity Set	Key Players	Impact	Progress Indicators Intangible	Progress Indicators Tangible
1. Customers	Changes to add to value delivered; ongoing delivery of value	Line	Make progress and make money	Feedback from customers	ACTION PLAN MILESTONES
2. Customers indirectly and the company	Employee relations; cost reductions for wider margins; basic research; investment decisions/ financing	Line and staff	Manage resources and save money	Company reputation	Customer-oriented operational measurements vs. targets
3. Company only	Tax, legal, and regulatory matters; community relations	Staff	Avoid trouble and avoid cost	INTERNAL OBSERVATIONS AND COMMENTS	Financial measurements vs. targets

to the outside world. The first place to look for tangible signs of progress is attainment of action plan milestones. Reaching even the first milestone denotes significant progress. Achieving successive action plan milestones automatically drives movement toward targeted performance for customers. For example:

▲ Revisions to current products give customers some of the performance characteristics they seek (ease of use, safety features, versatility, portability, low breakage, longer life), more of which will come with product redesign or new products.

▲ Procedural and paperwork changes in processing orders and preparing shipments reduce the turnaround time from order placement to shipment, which smoother materials flow through manufacturing will decrease even further.

Such advances in operational performance—although only approaching, not yet reaching, target levels—also trigger the reward system, especially since improvement on one measurement is being realized without detriment to others.

Progress during implementation can cause some cost-related movement toward financial targets. For example, revised manufacturing processes cause a decrease in parts to be reworked, reducing scrap and inventory write-offs. More complete shipments that are ready to leave on the date needed for surface transport avoid air shipment expenses. And fewer equipment breakdowns and shorter set-up times at production bottlenecks make it possible to adhere to the schedule without using overtime at downstream operations.

For actions requiring a long lead time, whose impact on operational measurements will show only when close to completion, a combination of plan milestones and customary financial controls is the main gauge of progress. Such actions include those to effect a major product innovation, make and integrate an acquisition, or prepare for entry into a significantly different customer segment.

For both long and shorter lead-time actions, the rate of progress is likely to be conspicuously faster than with past efforts to improve business performance—measured in weeks instead of months, or months instead of years. You'll probably find this personally rewarding, and you should. The people working on implementation may be the ones producing the progress, but the rate at which they're doing so is the direct result of your earlier efforts and of the help and encouragement you're providing.

▲   ▲   ▲

With implementation proceeding apace, and orientation to customers and organizational adjustments becoming embedded, you've completed the third part of Step Four. In the last part you continue to shepherd concerted action forward to achievement of financial targets.

Part D: Bottom-Line Benefits

You continue to lead concerted action to realize target levels of performance for customers and achieve financial targets, making the organizational and personnel changes that practical experience indicates are necessary. You screen employee suggestions and replan as needed based on market developments so as to sustain improved performance. Part D is highlighted in Figure 4-7.

▲   ▲   ▲

As successive milestones are passed, the distinction between implementation and day-to-day activities diminishes until the latter activities incorporate the effects of change and operational performance approaches target levels. This doesn't mean that you can relax. Turning your attention away from implementation would still be premature. And although current financial targets are being achieved, you need to consider further action to meet customers' changing needs, address other market developments, and sustain improved financial performance.

Putting on the Finishing Touches—for Now

Continuing to demonstrate your interest through everyday interactions maintains the momentum of implementation. Also, with your finger still on the pulse, you can tell when to intervene to keep concerted action on course—before a missed milestone jeopardizes attainment of targets.

As implementation moves from one phase to another, the team makeup is likely to evolve. For example, when a product revision approaches launch, the emphasis shifts from development to tasks related to supplying, marketing, and supporting the revision. Team leadership might naturally pass from one individual to another as implementation enters a new phase. Or you might find that a certain team leader's skills aren't developing as

Figure 4.-7. Step Four—The Culmination: Working Together for Customers and Profits, Part D.

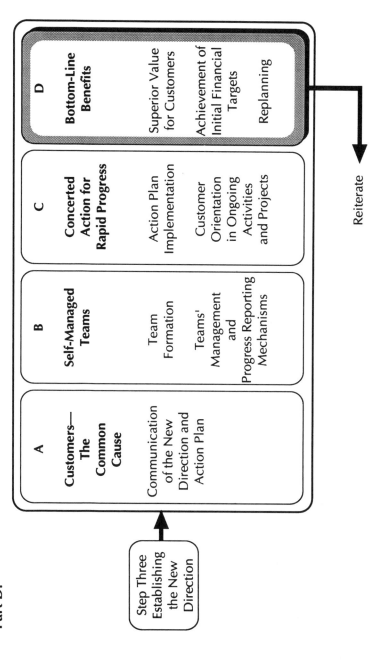

Step Three Establishing the New Direction

A

Customers— The Common Cause

Communication of the New Direction and Action Plan

B

Self-Managed Teams

Team Formation

Teams' Management and Progress Reporting Mechanisms

C

Concerted Action for Rapid Progress

Action Plan Implementation

Customer Orientation in Ongoing Activities and Projects

D

Bottom-Line Benefits

Superior Value for Customers

Achievement of Initial Financial Targets

Replanning

Reiterate

expected, or another leader is on the verge of burnout. Rotating leadership allows a respite from the most demanding role on a team, and it gives other people an opportunity to develop their skills.

Everyday interactions also reveal any roadblocks to customer-oriented teamwork becoming the norm. It may be that some people can't or won't go along with the new direction, work more collaboratively, or guide and support their staff rather than issue commands and play on their fears. When simple discussion with the individual is ineffective in improving such behavior, skills training can obviate the need for more drastic measures such as reassignment to tasks requiring less teamwork or a position without supervisory responsibility.

Assessing the impact of organizational adjustments indicates where refinement is needed. The more effective the organizational infrastructure, the less you need do to sustain the impact of the special stimulus you provided early in implementation. When reviewing the effectiveness of adjustments already made, you might find, for example, that engineering's redefined role (emphasizing customer-defined product characteristics and ease-of-manufacture at a certain cost rather than technological sophistication) is not taking root. Creating a manufacturing engineering department that includes some people currently in engineering would remove a remaining structural hurdle.

You might find that the reward system needs further adjustments. This was the case at a company that had instituted a complimentary dinner for two as a way for managers to recognize outstanding individual efforts. The idea was altered to include the employee's whole family in the outing, up to a specified amount.

Since poor administration of a reward system deters productive action and high morale, you need to make certain that the adjustments you defined are being adhered to. Overseeing fair distribution of rewards is another task without end. Failure to guard against poor administration risks deterioration into outright abuse, such as grading individual performance to tie in with predetermined distribution of rewards. Periodic pay increases, bonuses, and promotions must go to the people who are known to be high-performing contributors. Whenever rewards go to people other than high performers, those who do perform well feel undervalued, and people throughout the organization read a strong negative signal.

Ensuring that people receive the right signals helps make orientation to customers and bottom-line results take root firmly and eventually become standard operating procedure. Communicating progress to date provides feedback to people throughout the organization and lets them see that concerted action is bearing fruit—and that you are aware of and pleased with this fact.

Hearing Good News From Customers

Passing the last milestones of the action plan leads to the changes being absorbed into day-to-day delivery of products and services to customers. A revised product becomes part of your regular product line, forecasts are updated regularly, streamlined procedures to respond to customer inquiries are followed as a matter of course, or more flexible billing terms are offered as a standard option. As this integration occurs, operational performance reaches target levels. This is cause for rejoicing, especially when customers notice the improvement in company performance. Progress now shows in indicators other than action plan milestones and internal observation and comments, as shown in capitals in Figure 4-8.

Customers' favorable reactions can reach you in various ways. A customer you meet at an industry convention might comment on the improvement in company performance. But people who have frequent contact with customers will be the first to detect a decrease in complaints. This good news should be shared. At one company, two customers asked the account manager to be sure to relay their appreciation. The people involved in implementation were delighted to hear this.

The newly positive views of customers that routinely assess their suppliers will show in how they grade and rank your company. As the industry grapevine spreads the good word, your company's enhanced reputation will help you obtain new business.

Figure 4-8. Evidence of progress.

Priority/Key Beneficiary	Activity Set	Impact	Progress Indicators	
			Intangible	Tangible
1. Customers	Changes to add to value delivered; ongoing delivery of value	Make progress and make money	FEEDBACK FROM CUSTOMERS	Action plan milestones
2. Customers indirectly and the company	Employee relations; cost reductions for wider margins; basic research; investment decisions/ financing	Manage resources and save money	COMPANY REPUTA-TION	CUSTOMER-ORIENTED OPERA-TIONAL MEASURE-MENTS vs. targets
3. Company only	Tax, legal, and regula-tory matters; community relations	Avoid trouble and avoid cost	Internal observation and com-ments	FINANCIAL MEASURE-MENTS vs. targets

Seeing the Ultimate Proof: Profit Gains and Higher Returns

Hearing that your company is admired and possibly envied is gratifying. So is knowing that you're mastering whatever business issue you set out to resolve. But, as the saying goes, you can't take these things to the bank. The ultimate proof of effective planning and action is profit improvement and, more specifically, achievement of financial targets, for both profitability and investment returns. Serving customers more effectively is a major accomplishment, but it's only half the battle. Doing so more profitably is the other half.

Let's say that in a customer segment you're focusing on, your company now outperforms almost every other supplier. Matching or exceeding the performance of the top suppliers makes your company one of the elite few—indeed, you may actually have achieved the top ranking. Providing greater value (than the second-tier suppliers or than your company did in the past) means customers will be increasing the portion of their business they do with you, causing revenue to move toward target levels.

Many companies point to revenue growth or market share gains as showing improved business performance, as if these figures told the whole story. Yet revenue growth of 2 percent in a market growing at 5 percent is nothing to write home about. Nor is an increase in operating profit of 3 percent on revenue growth of 6 percent. Such a result means that each *new* dollar in sales contributes *less* to profits than do current sales dollars.

A revenue gain achieved with the same level of resources drops straight to the bottom line—after, of course, subtracting costs directly related to higher unit volumes, such as those for purchased materials. That bottom-line increase lifts investment returns. But an increase in profits that is less than the increase in revenue indicates that existing resources are being *less* productively deployed than before, or that the addition of resources has actually reduced profitability as a percentage of sales. In either case, the return on invested capital is actually *lower* than before.

Such results aren't good enough for tough-minded, truly bottom-line-oriented executives and others who track and examine company performance, such as investors. They look for operating profit that's a *higher* percentage of sales revenue than in the past. More impressive still is profit growth greater than the growth of demand in the relevant customer segment. Such profit growth is evidence that a company's direction—where it does business (which customer segments it focuses on) and how it performs for customers there (which value elements it emphasizes)—is doubly effective: This direction is enabling the company to take business from competitors *and* make the most of its current strengths and resources.

Having financial information that breaks out operating profit by customer segment makes it easy to tell that the profits generated there (revenue less all costs related to sales, marketing, manufacture, distribution, service, administration, and product development) are moving toward or meeting targets. For example:

▲ At a company whose customer segments include consumer mass marketers purchasing customized products, achievement of the profit targeted for that segment started six months after implementation began. This was achieved primarily by advancing performance on the Transaction to correct a weakness and by subsequently increasing prices, which customers accepted.

▲ In a business unit supplying specialty chemicals for large-scale industrial operations, advancing performance on the Product built on the company's established strength on the Transaction and Support in one of the few customer segments with high growth. Tailoring a current product for this segment in a way that decreased the cash cost of manufacture generated almost all (80 percent) of the business unit's profit growth (30 percent) over a two-year period. The increase in profit from this customer segment exceeded the increase in revenue generated there and the growth in demand there.

▲ At a company involved in a number of industries, a division making aircraft components met its profit plan in the first and succeeding years. Profit targets for the first year were achieved while attaining action plan milestones and customer-oriented operational targets. This led to achieving later years' profit targets. Again, profit growth exceeded revenue growth and the market growth rate. Return on total capital invested in this division rose from 17 percent to 23 percent. Moreover, division management observed that rigorous planning had produced profit targets that were more realistic, reducing the need for make-the-numbers maneuvers to meet the profit plan.

Achieving profit targets is, of course, the supreme cause for celebration and reward. The time has come for congratulations all around. In addition to personal recognition and hoopla, any monetary rewards (stock options, bonuses) tied to business performance can now be distributed.

Reaping the Benefits of Culture Change

Life goes on after the cheering has faded, but a return to business as usual is not a viable option. Implementation of longer lead-time actions must continue. Fostering unity of purpose and orientation to customers never ends. And it's a certainty that new opportunities and problems will present themselves and need to be addressed. Such considerations create the need to replan—to determine what else the company or business unit should work on or what it should work on next—and then take action accordingly.

You have accomplished something that will stand the company in good stead: a change in culture. The organization as a whole has closed ranks and operated as a cohesive entity, adapting to change and innovating successfully. This means that it's now more agile and better able to cope quickly and effectively with what the future brings. With this ability comes added confidence, which breeds a can-do attitude and a renewed willingness to strive and try new ways.

Cultural change—a much-sought-after phenomenon—is commonly referred to as if it were an action item or an objective, but it is actually a consequence. Of greatest significance to you and other executives is the fact that less momentum is needed to move the organization into successively higher gears.

Greater openness to change and keener interest in customers and the company's welfare have a number of effects. At one company, long-standing resistance to a productivity increase concept evaporated. This concept called for one operator to run two machines at the same time. Operators took it upon themselves to explore how to make this concept work and, with the help of engineers, succeeded.

More and better suggestions are likely. The fact that people throughout the organization now have a clearer understanding of what constitutes a good idea, and people at lower levels now see that their insight and contributions are valued, prompts excellent suggestions from various places. Someone in sales might propose a combination of specific products from different product lines to meet customer needs over time or in particular circumstances. Someone in finance might suggest a way to sort billing information to tie in with customers' accounting systems.

Not all ideas will be workable, of course, and some will be more worthwhile than others. Sound suggestions involving minor resource commitments can be put into effect with little analysis. But other ideas need more thorough examination, which also helps determine which suggestions to pursue first.

Selecting the suggestions of benefit to customers and to the company is a simple matter. Reviewing internal suggestions based on overall direction defined in terms of customers indicates which ideas are most relevant to them. Suggestions that tie in with product and service attributes valued by key customers can be determined in light of the conclusions of Part A, Which Customers? How to Attract and Keep Them? of Step Three—The Crux: Establishing the New Direction.

For ideas that do offer significant benefit for customers, you can gauge the financial benefit to the company by working through Part C, Practical Matters—Actions, Timing, and Resources, of Step Two—Concreteness: Scoping Out Needed Changes. If the figures are satisfactory and implementation relatively extensive, development of an action plan would follow, as in Part B, Blueprint for Action, of Step Three. This would give you the basis to revise resource allocations and financial targets.

Maintaining Your Company's Lead Through Replanning

Replanning is done by using the CORe Method iteratively. There are two types of reiteration: (1) determining whether a radical new possibility that presents itself offers the company a real opportunity, and (2) defining opportunities on the basis of market developments.

New Possibilities. Decisions about which customer segments to do business in and invest in and how best to position the company there are likely to remain valid for the foreseeable future. But radically new possibilities that present themselves can involve revising those decisions or a current target market position. Such a possibility might be:

▲ The sudden availability at a fire-sale price of a potential acquisition candidate, or an approach by a desirable ally for joint product development or marketing. Either of these could offer a way to obtain the capabilities needed to succeed in an attractive customer segment you don't currently serve.

▲ A technological breakthrough in your R&D or manufacturing operations. This could offer a way to provide customers with another key product attribute, or an entirely new product, that would be of real benefit to them. This suggests redefining the current target market position.

However, knowing what it would take to capitalize on such a new possibility is vital to determining on a factual and rational basis whether it's worth pursuing. Without an assessment of what a new possibility would entail in the way of time and resources, any thought of changing the current direction would be a waste of time, probably produce faulty decisions, and risk upsetting the company's current plans and activities for no good reason. What appears at first to be an opportunity can actually be more conceptually appealing than pragmatically feasible and financially worthwhile.

Should the new possibility apply to a market area you didn't explore in Step One—The Context: Understanding Customer Viewpoints, or if a significant time has gone by since doing that analysis, you'd need to do at least parts of Step One. With up-to-date information on the customer segment and competitors, you'd then need to subject the new possibility to the scrutiny of Part C, Practical Matters—Actions, Timing, and Resources, of Step Two. Using the information this produces, you can work through as much of Step Three as necessary to tell (1) whether the new possibility is one whose absolute merits warrant pursuing it and (2) whether its merits relative to the company's current plans and activities warrant taking resources away from them or adding resources. As before, this is likely to take some iteration.

Should the new possibility pass these tests, you'd then complete Step Three to make all the needed preparations before embarking on implementation.

Market Developments. To a front-runner, market developments can be an opportunity; to a slow mover, both the developments themselves and the front-runner's actions present a problem. Slow movers can only *re* act. Watching out for and reviewing market developments as they occur lets you detect early any opportunities to capitalize on the company's enhanced capabilities or when defensive action may be called for.

Your success with customers is likely to prompt at least some retaliation from competitors. The less alert competitors won't detect the threat you represent until the evidence shows in their lost orders. But a smarter competitor that's attentive to customers' views has probably been monitoring what your company is doing and will soon learn of its new standing in customers' eyes. Such a competitor may have countermeasures ready to put into effect.

As the saying goes, the best defense is a good offense. Knowing when this is called for requires early warning. Continual monitoring and review of market developments provide early indication of a competitor's retaliation, giving you time to determine whether, when, and how to respond.

Staying abreast of market developments that affect customers lets you take preemptive action, obviating the need to replan merely for purposes of defense. Several types of market development revealed by continual monitoring can trigger replanning to stay ahead of the game. For example:

▲ Review of publicly available information might reveal that a trend is shifting direction or gathering strength, such as when health-conscious consumers started seeking fitness equipment for home use.
▲ Updates from everyday interactions with customers let you get early insight into how their plans and priorities are changing.

Conducting another round of customer interviews reveals in a concrete and credible way whether your reading of trends or deductions from informal updates corresponds with customers' views.

New information about customers or competitors obtained through market monitoring doesn't automatically imply a need to replan. When a customer makes an acquisition, your company's status as a preferred supplier is at little risk. It's the second-tier suppliers of both the acquiring and the acquired company that have a problem. Changes that customers make or events that affect competitors may also not imply a need to replan. If a customer is cutting back on the number of suppliers it uses, those that remain on the list—where your company is now close to the top—get a larger share of that customer's business.

Keeping an Eye on the Future

Meeting periodically and expressly to keep an eye on the horizon with customers uppermost in mind has considerable advantages for the company's future prosperity. These include:

▲ Increasing the chances of anticipating changes in customer needs and competitors' actions instead of having to deduce from harder-to-get or lost orders that it's time to take action—to *react*
▲ Refining direction in a logical way to keep building on current strengths, minimize the need for additional capital, and avoid unwarranted risk
▲ Establishing an early and strong position in an emerging market area

In each of these instances, you leave the less-attractive markets and also-ran positions for other companies to make of what they can. Your company moves from strength to strength, continuing to provide superior value for customers and achieve outstanding financial results.

▲   ▲   ▲

Having achieved profit targets for shorter lead-time actions, identified when to revisit earlier steps, and arranged when the management team will meet to stay ahead of the game, you've completed the last part of Step Four.

You have also arrived at the end of the CORe Method. Now that you know what it consists of and how the parts fit together, the next logical questions are about applying it in your business. How to get started is covered in the next section.

Recap of Step Four—The Culmination

In Step Four, you realized the benefits of what was done in the preceding steps, setting in motion and leading the accomplishment of customer-oriented changes. These changes resulted in the company providing superior value for current and new customers, making more productive use of all its resources, and achieving its financial targets.

The orientation to customers and bottom-line results embodied in the new direction influenced the way work is done on day-to-day activities and other projects. As a result, the organization as a whole is now more cohesive and better able to accomplish change quickly and effectively to continue providing exceptional value for customers and exceptional profits for the company.

Figure 4-9 shows what was done in Step Four.

Figure 4-9. Step Four—The Culmination: Working Together for Customers and Profits, recap.

Part	What You Achieved and How
A Customers—The Common Cause	Spread understanding of customers, the new direction and action plan, and revised priorities and resource allocations by: ▲ Conducting discussions at all levels and in all functions
B Self-Managed Teams	Organized the implementation teams and built their sense of ownership and responsibility for progress by: ▲ Forming the teams and ensuring that they understood their responsibilities, including self-management ▲ Having the teams develop detailed work plans and define mechanisms to track and report progress
C Concerted Action for Rapid Progress	Initiated action plan implementation and ensured that it received the support it needed and that progress is recognized by: ▲ Monitoring team progress against action plan milestones ▲ Responding to team requests for guidance or intervention, providing encouragement in person and appreciation of effort and achievement ▲ Making sure ongoing activities and other projects proceed in keeping with the new direction and priorities and that customer orientation and teamwork are becoming entrenched
D Bottom-Line Benefits	Delivered superior value for customers and outstanding financial results for the company by: ▲ Continuing to shepherd implementation toward targeted performance for customers and initial financial targets, making organizational refinements as needed ▲ Ensuring that recognition and reward distribution reflect outstanding results-oriented effort and performance ▲ Monitoring market, customer, and competitor developments and replanning as needed ▲ Taking further action to remain a leading supplier in attractive customer segments, capitalize on company strengths, and thereby sustain the increase in profitability and investment returns

SECTION III
THE APPLICATION

Because it is so versatile, there's no one right way or right time to use the CORe Method. The primary application is *problem solving*—that is, to improve financial performance by resolving a specific, general management issue. Other applications are *decision making* (when, for example, evaluating plans and proposals prior to giving approval—or thinking through any particularly complex decision) and *strategic planning* (when, for example, developing and implementing a business unit's strategic plan).

When several issues affect the same customers, it's more considerate to them—and more efficient for you—to address the issues together. Addressing multiple issues at the same time is the equivalent of planning strategically as and when needed rather than on a preset schedule. When business issues require here-and-now attention, the work you do on them with the CORe Method gives you a leg up on the next round of planning. In fact, there's no reason that strategic planning couldn't be the first use. Whether addressing one or several new issues or doing strategic planning, the CORe Method serves as a complete road map.

If work on a particular issue is already under way, you can use the CORe Method as a checklist to reveal any key omissions in what's been done so far and the tasks needed to fill in the gaps. When deciding on major resource commitments, referring to this checklist prompts questions to determine whether a particular proposal is complete, internally consistent, and detailed enough about needed actions and resource requirements for you to have confidence in the results projected.

Figure III-1 depicts the CORe Method in a format for use as a checklist. This layout also serves as a guide when using the method as a whole. This Section is about that full use, not just conceptual use such as when you are thinking through a decision.

Introducing the CORe Method at Your Company

How best to introduce the CORe Method at your company and in what level of detail is a matter for the management team or business unit to decide. Using the CORe Method fully and efficiently calls for an orderly effort masterminded from the top of the business unit—in most cases by the general manager. Other members of the management team must, however, agree to or at least go along with use of the CORe Method. By its nature, CORe calls for the active participation of several functions. Nods that carry the greatest weight are from sales, R&D (or engineering), and manufacturing (or operations, including purchasing, materials management, quality assurance, and so on). These functions' contributions and early involvement are critical for successful implementation.

It's unnecessary to refer explicitly to the CORe Method when introducing it to middle and lower levels. It may be better to play down the fact that a specific tool is involved to avoid the suspicion that this is just another management fad. Describing the approach without referring specifically to the CORe Method is straightforward and appeals to logic: "In order to solve this problem, we need to know more about customers—what their prospects and priorities are. By understanding what matters most to them, we can find out what it would take for us to provide it. That way, we'll have the facts to make a sound decision. If we decide to go forward, we'll know what we're getting into and what financial benefits we can expect." You can always reveal later, when the novelty has worn off, that the approach used is a method that is documented and has a name.

Identifying the Key Players for Steps One and Two

The first consideration in getting started is, who will do the work in Step One—The Context: Understanding Customer Viewpoints and Step Two—Concreteness: Scoping Out Needed Changes? The key players in Step Three—The Crux: Establishing the New Direction are a given: the business unit management team. Included in Step Three is the decision on who else will be involved and in what role in Step Four—The Culmination: Working Together for Customers and Profits.

There are two basic arrangements for doing Steps One and Two. You can either make work on the CORe Method part of people's day-to-day jobs or set up a small dedicated task force. For either arrangement, you might use a combination of company people and some outside consulting help. Having outsiders work side by side with company people is essential. When outsiders work independently, what they come up with is likely to be perceived as *their* answer. This automatically implies a lack of internal ownership.

For each of these arrangements, it must be made clear who is responsible for leading the work. Designating one person to become your in-house expert on the CORe Method and its use has considerable merit. However, this individual must have certain qualifications:

▲ Analytical proficiency—experience with analytical work and a keen mind

▲ Proven project leadership skills—a certain amount of initiative

▲ Personal credibility with people at various levels—a level of trustworthiness and discretion

▲ Knowledge of company activities and operations—a certain amount of time with the company

▲ A broad business perspective and an open mind—a point of view not limited by expertise in any one function, an orientation to results, and a certain level of personal security

The rarest of these qualifications is proficiency in market analysis, even in well-established companies. Many companies

(*Text continues on page 226.*)

Figure III-1. The CORe™ Management Method checklist.

Step One—The Context: Understanding Customer Viewpoints

Part	Name	Description	Procedures	✓
A	Bird's-Eye View of the Market	Determine what lies ahead for customers and your company	Map out supply chain to/from end users Interpret market forces and trends	
B	The High-Potential Customers	Identify the types of customers that offer the best profit potential for your company	Define customer segments in terms of distinctive buying factors and their weight using customer value elements Assess segments for profit potential, specifying which to explore in depth	
C	Customers' Viewpoint	Learn from customers the product and service attributes they value most, their plans, and their view of supplier strengths and weaknesses	Select customers to interview Prepare for interviews Conduct survey	
D	Customer Orientation of Competitors	Determine likely changes in key competitors' performance for customers and competitors' likely actions	Evaluate key competitors' performance improvement efforts Identify probable drivers of competitors' future actions/reactions	

Step Two—Concreteness: Scoping Out Needed Changes

Part	Name	Description	Procedures	✓
A	Company Skills to Look Into	Specify the customer-defined product and service attributes to be analyzed	Review customer interview results in light of current business issues and the likely feasibility of innovations	
B	Needed Changes and Ways to Make Them	Define approaches to accomplish the changes needed to provide specific product and service attributes	Determine reasons for gap between customer value sought/provided Develop approaches to address these reasons	
C	Practical Matters: Actions, Timing, and Resources	Determine what it's going to take to put needed changes into practice	Identify implementation actions in all functions Gauge timing and resources, including any capabilities needed/lacking and time/money trade-off options	
D	Consolidated Findings	Validate approaches and implementation requirements	Review findings with the people who developed them	

Copyright © 1993 Lindsay Geddes

Step Three—The Crux: Establishing the New Direction*

Part	Name	Description	Procedures
A	Which Customers? How to Attract and Keep Them?	Determine customer segment importance to your company and define its target position	Review customer prospects and viewpoints, competitive situation, and implementation requirements to ascertain customer segment potential for profits and returns Determine customer value elements to emphasize in light of implementation requirements and competitors' capabilities
B	Blueprint for Action	Develop an action plan to guide implementation throughout the organization	Lay out time-phased action plan for all functions Annotate with resource requirements, including key people
C	Resources for Customers, Profits for the Company	Revise resource allocations and overall priorities in light of the new direction and agree on the best possible financial targets	Reallocate existing resources to customer-oriented changes and other key topics, specifying activities with lower priorities Calculate financial outcomes, refining resource allocations as necessary and revising action plan timing accordingly
D	Setting the Stage	Adjust the organizational infrastructure to encourage smooth and effective implementation	Review and define adjustments to roles/responsibilities, organizational structure, business performance measurements, and the reward system
E	Management Team Sanction	Solidify commitment to lead concerted action and to realize targeted results	Review and approve the new direction and related decisions, ensuring that documentation is clear and brief

Step Four—The Culmination: Working Together for Customers and Profits

Part	Name	Description	Procedures
A	Customers: The Common Cause	Spread understanding of the new direction, the action plan, and revised priorities and resource allocations	Conduct discussions in all functions and at all levels
B	Self-Managed Teams	Organize implementation teams, building their sense of ownership and responsibility for progress	Form teams and have them define self-management tools and reporting mechanisms
C	Concerted Action for Rapid Progress	Initiate implementation, ensuring that it receives adequate support and that progress is recognized	Implement the action plan, tracking progress against milestones Pursue ongoing activities/projects according to revised priorities
D	Bottom-Line Benefits	Deliver superior value to customers to produce and sustain outstanding financial results	Achieve operational and financial targets Monitor market developments and replan

*Step Three is iterative.

have people who can do operational, technical, and financial analysis and can analyze market data. However, analyzing market data and analyzing a market are different undertakings. The ability to gather information (via market research projects, from the sales force and publications, through discussions with industry experts) isn't enough. Many a researcher and/or person with the job title of analyst is highly skilled at obtaining, compiling, and manipulating data, but such activities differ from interpreting data to extract meaning and determine conclusions of business significance. It is this interpretation that produces dependable information on which to base your decisions. Presenting the key conclusions clearly and succinctly is also a hallmark of proficiency in market analysis.

Doing the analysis and directing it are different tasks. Directing analytical work is a type of project leadership. An organization that customarily uses cross-functional teams may have a number of people who are able to play a project leadership role and who have the personal credibility to do so effectively. A line manager who takes part in collaborative efforts—rather than supervises tasks and instructs people—and who has a business perspective and an entrepreneurial bent makes an excellent project leader. However, a person who's at his or her best in a position of command in a structured environment with narrow scope is unlikely to be effective—or comfortable—in a project leadership role, which involves communicating with people who have different areas of expertise, coalescing multiple perspectives, and shepherding activities forward without direct authority.

A person who's adept at staff work may lack the sense of urgency and visible resolve needed to get the work completed promptly. Attention to detail is vital, but getting mired in it and emphasizing cosmetics over content impedes progress. Thus, researchers, planners, or analysts may be well-qualified to *do* the work in Steps One and Two, but may not be suitable to *direct* that work. You might, however, have a suitable person who happens to be in a staff position, is frustrated there, and is eager to show what he or she can do in a more results-oriented role.

Different people might be best suited to lead the work in Step One and Step Two. The nature of the work in these steps differs, and an individual's strengths are likely to apply more to either market analysis (Step One) or internal analysis and identification of implementation requirements (Step Two).

Depending on the scope you define for Step Two, you might need two or more people to spearhead the work in it. You need as many team leaders as there are value elements being explored. Trying to guide more than one team when each is working on a different value element can get confusing for even a highly experienced person. You won't know, of course, until you get into Step Two how many teams there'll be and, therefore, how many team leaders are needed.

The choice of who takes the project leadership role in Step One also depends on how you're using the CORe Method. For example, if you're using it for a new product introduction, a marketing manager would be a prime candidate; if you're using it to develop or update the business plan, the head of marketing might be the best choice. Whoever directs the work, he or she must be solely and directly answerable for it to the general manager. This is especially so for the market analysis work (Step One).

The person directing the market analysis probably needs to be assigned full time, unless Step One represents only a more rigorous or integrated version of your company's current practices. A part-time effort is workable when, for example, you already have most of the raw data or already have customer segments properly defined. However, when the front end of the CORe Method differs considerably from current practices, you may have to face the fact that the analytical expertise and leadership skills needed to do a good job of Step One and, possibly, Step Two are either not available in-house or not available in adequate supply.

Considering Outside Help

Should you need, or merely want to consider, using outside help to speed the process, there are certain characteristics to look for in a consulting firm. These characteristics are essentially the same as the qualifications listed above for inside experts, but with some different connotations. These are:

▲ Analytical proficiency—experience in the work called for, such as market segmentation and the design and execution of customer interview programs

▲ Proven project leadership skills—and the flexibility to share the leadership role with company people
▲ Personal credibility, with people at various levels—an operating background and at least several years of work experience
▲ Knowledge of company activities and operations—industry knowledge and hands-on operating experience
▲ A broad business perspective and an open mind—a point of view not limited by specialization, whether in a particular function, industry, or type of consulting or solution, an orientation to results, and a certain level of personal security

Assuming the requisite analytical expertise, the most important things to look for are broad business perspective and operating experience.

What's needed is a firm that consults *on* management rather than one that consults *to* management. People who have not managed in an operating business cannot know what that really means or entails. And people who have never had to take a general management perspective are less likely to think in terms of bottom-line results.

What you're looking for, therefore, is this: People who can help you come up with—in the quickest and most cost-effective way, using an overall methodology of your choosing—the key information needed for you to figure out what the best course of action is in your present situation. Consultants who are willing to roll up their sleeves and work with people in various parts of the organization and at all levels provide extra resources to augment your in-house capabilities. Such consultants also help your people to learn, sharing skills that will be useful in the future.

You are not looking for a firm that's in the business of producing reports. Many consulting firms specialize in certain areas, such as competitive analysis, customer surveys, organizational studies, and operational analysis. Such assistance is invaluable in certain circumstances, but you don't need copious, beautifully produced documents or outsiders' recommended solutions. Nor are you looking for a consulting firm that specializes in a particular functional area or a predefined improvement program. You already have functional specialists and implementors in-house. Moreover, you won't know until you have the results of customer interviews which specialties are relevant. When the key issue for customers is product performance characteristics, expertise in materials flow, productivity, design of sales promotions, or the customer service function will be of little help.

Before assuming that you need outside help, further reading on the parts of the CORe Method that are newest to your company might allow you to get started without it. You can decide later—but not so late as to risk a false start—whether you need outside help at all. (A list of subjects and sources for further reading is located after Section III.) If you think outside help might be needed, compile a shortlist of appropriate firms to give yourself a safety net. You can then bring in assistance on short notice.

Even when you have an adequate supply of the relevant expertise in-house, there can be advantages to engaging some outside help. The most important consideration is the quality of information produced by customer interviews. People at a customer company are often more likely to share information freely and objectively with a credible third party than with a company employee. Having an outsider involved also helps maintain objectivity. Yesterday's set-in-stone assumptions can be more easily exposed by a fresh view. And a clear-thinking, level-headed person to act as a sounding board can be a real asset during your deliberations on future direction. Such a person can also help you keep up the momentum and be a source of morale support for tough, far-reaching decisions.

Estimating Overall Timing and What Drives It

Just as each company and each situation is unique, so is each application of the CORe Method. Thus, the timing varies from one application to the next. The timing of Step Four—The Culmination: Working Together for Customers and Profits is determined in Step Three—The Crux: Establishing the New Direction. Thus, the only general statement about the time involved applies to the first three steps: From the start of Step One—The Context: Understanding Customer Viewpoints through the completion of Step Three usually takes three to six months, with four or five being average.

Assume that you'll have the work led by people inside the company and either have enough people in-house with the requisite knowledge, skills, and traits to do the work, or you'll have some assistance from well-chosen outsiders. In these circumstances, the four or five months would then break down approximately as follows:

▲ Step One starts in the first week and takes six to eight weeks through completion of the customer interviews. The competitive analysis takes a few weeks more but, done in parallel with Step Two and finishing before it does, doesn't affect overall timing.
▲ Step Two starts in the seventh to ninth week (after the customer interviews) and takes six weeks.
▲ Step Three starts immediately after completion of Step Two, in the thirteenth to fifteenth week, and can take from two to six weeks.

With sufficient research and analytical expertise and adequate staffing for Steps One and Two, the other key determinants of timing are as follows:

Step One—The Context: Understanding Customer Viewpoints

▲ How well-documented the industry is and how much of this publicly available information you already have on hand
▲ How complete, up-to-date, accurate, and organized is existing internally generated information on customers and competitors
▲ The number and size of the customer segments in which you'll conduct interviews

Step Two—Concreteness: Scoping Out Needed Changes

▲ Management team members' schedules
▲ The degree of novelty—for example, determining what's involved in developing an all-new product is likely to take longer than exploring a product revision
▲ The involvement of entities outside the business unit, such as another division, materials suppliers, and regulatory authorities

Step Three—The Crux: Establishing the New Direction

▲ Management team members' schedules and how accustomed they are to working as a team
▲ The availability of number-crunching expertise
▲ The extent of any organizational adjustments

With a concentrated effort, Step Three need take only two or three weeks. But, in addition to the determinants listed, you need time to reflect. This is especially so when defining overall direction and priorities in terms of customers for the first time. And the time needed to define organizational adjustments in light of revised priorities is impossible to predict. Four to six weeks for Step Three could, therefore, be more realistic. It makes no sense to rush through decisions about the company's future direction and preparations to pursue it successfully just to save a couple of weeks.

The degree of business unit autonomy can also affect timing. If a major investment is involved, or there's a company requirement for approval prior to implementation, this can delay completion of Step Three.

Another general determinant of elapsed time for the first three steps is the need to keep the business going. This is a consideration even though the CORe Method streamlines the front-end analytical work. Despite this built-in efficiency, the fact that almost all company personnel will have other responsibilities can affect the timing. Rarely is someone assigned full time to work on the CORe Method. This means that real-world imperatives are sometimes going to take precedence. These imperatives include serving today's customers, achieving the current profit plan, doing payroll, and preparing the quarterly financial statement.

The probable timing for Steps One, Two, and Three, and who in the company is most intensely involved at what stage, are shown in Figure III-2.

Projecting the probable timing for Step Four—The Culmination: Working Together for Customers and Profits in the abstract is speculation. The timing can be known with certainty only after you are well into Step Three—The Crux: Establishing the New Direction, that is, after you've defined direction and the action plan to pursue it has been laid out. However, the general determinants of Step Four timing are:

Figure III-2. Key players' involvement in each part of the CORe™ Management Method.

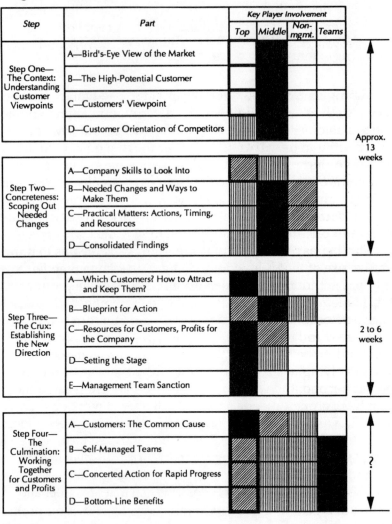

Step	Part	Key Player Involvement			
		Top	Middle	Non-mgmt.	Teams
Step One—The Context: Understanding Customer Viewpoints	A—Bird's-Eye View of the Market		Heavy		
	B—The High-Potential Customer		Heavy		
	C—Customers' Viewpoint		Heavy		
	D—Customer Orientation of Competitors	Minor	Heavy		
Step Two—Concreteness: Scoping Out Needed Changes	A—Company Skills to Look Into	Moderate	Minor		
	B—Needed Changes and Ways to Make Them	Minor	Heavy	Moderate	
	C—Practical Matters: Actions, Timing, and Resources	Minor	Heavy	Moderate	
	D—Consolidated Findings	Minor	Heavy		
Step Three—The Crux: Establishing the New Direction	A—Which Customers? How to Attract and Keep Them?	Heavy	Minor		
	B—Blueprint for Action	Moderate	Heavy	Minor	
	C—Resources for Customers, Profits for the Company	Heavy	Moderate		
	D—Setting the Stage	Heavy	Minor		
	E—Management Team Sanction	Heavy			
Step Four—The Culmination: Working Together for Customers and Profits	A—Customers: The Common Cause	Heavy	Moderate	Minor	
	B—Self-Managed Teams	Moderate	Minor		Heavy
	C—Concerted Action for Rapid Progress	Moderate	Minor	Minor	Heavy
	D—Bottom-Line Benefits	Moderate	Minor		Heavy

Approx. 13 weeks (Step One and Step Two)

2 to 6 weeks (Step Three)

? (Step Four)

Key:
Top: General manager and functional heads
Middle: People reporting to functional heads; other salaried people
Non-mgmt.: Nonmanagement
Teams: Implementation team members, including leaders, at any level

□ = Primary responsibility   ■ = Heavy   ▨ = Moderate   ▥ = Minor   □ = None

▲ The amount of newness, such as a new market area or all-new product
▲ The degree of collaboration needed with other parties (another division, joint venture partner, suppliers)
▲ How accustomed the company is to teamwork and innovation

Timing of Step Four also varies with how you're using the CORe Method. A company reversing poor relationships with current customers completed implementation and saw the profit impact within nine months after the start of Step Four. At another company which had done its strategic business plan more rigorously than ever before, the first intense phase of its action plan covered eighteen months, during which time the profit plan was met. Uncertainty about the timing of Step Four is outweighed by the greater certainty of its outcome.

Another aspect of timing that is unpredictable has to do with iterative use of the CORe Method. As described in Step Four, one such use is the monitoring of market developments during and after implementation, which can call for looping back to earlier steps to determine whether and how to respond. Or Step One may be repeated to take a fresh look at, for example, how customer needs and priorities are changing and how the competitive situation is evolving. As with any activity, the learning curve concept applies: Second and subsequent iterations are likely to be quicker than the first one.

Getting Started

Using the CORe Method as a complete road map doesn't mean that you have to generate all information from scratch. You probably already have information about trends in your industry. Sales reps and field service people are likely to know how distinctions among customer types affect what they look for in a supplier. And people in various parts of the company are likely to know bits and pieces about certain competitors. You may, therefore, already have a wealth of market information—some of it in people's heads and some on paper, some of it up-to-date and reliable and some older and less accurate. Thus, the first task for the people working on Step One is to collect and compile information that already exists. To do so, they need the right work space. Market analysis is hard work that requires concentration. It's important, therefore, that a place be provided where distractions and unwarranted interruptions are few and what's being worked on can be left undisturbed.

Having assembled the information, the next task is to organize and review it and identify any holes. For example, points made in sales call reports can be a good indicator of what's of concern to current customers, but they do not necessarily indicate the viewpoint of a new customer segment. They may also lack objectivity.

When filling holes in existing information or verifying it, there's little reason to pay for a consultant, should you be using one, to collect publicly available information. Doing a literature search, obtaining annual reports from companies or reports from government bodies, and looking up industry statistics in the library are all tasks that company people can perform.

Published information and, possibly, information from people knowledgeable about specific industries is enough to do Part A, Bird's-Eye View of the Market and Part B, The High-Potential Customer of Step One—The Context: Understanding Customer Viewpoints. In Part C, Customers' Viewpoint, information comes from customers themselves and guides the information gathered in Part D, Customer Orientation of Competitors. Part D probably requires collecting additional data, either in greater depth about a company known to be a competitor or about a company not formerly identified as such.

By the time you have people working on evaluating the key competitors, you and other members of the management team will be using the results of customer interviews to define the focus of the work in Step Two—Concreteness: Scoping Out Needed Changes. At this point, you're no longer getting started but are well on your way with the CORe Method—and well on your way toward providing superior value for customers and realizing higher profits and returns for the company.

Subjects and Sources for Further Reading

Chapters are identified in most sources in order to highlight those of particular relevance to a specific step.

Step One—The Context: Understanding Customer Viewpoints

Subjects	Sources
Industry and market analysis, market segmentation, competitive analysis	B. Charles Ames and James D. Hlavacek. *Managerial Marketing: The Ultimate Advantage.* Mountainside, N.J.: Managerial Marketing, Inc., 1984. Chapters 3, 4, 5, 6. Peter F. Drucker. *Managing for Results.* New York: Harper & Row, 1964, 1986. Chapter 6. Kenichi Ohmae. *The Mind of the Strategist.* New York: McGraw-Hill, 1982. Chapter 9. Jack Savidge, *Marketing Intelligence: Discover What Your Customers Really Want and What Your Competitors Are Up to.* Homewood, Ill.: Business One Irwin, 1992. Chapters 5, 6, 7.

Step Two—Concreteness: Scoping Out Needed Changes

Subjects	Sources
Participative management, problem analysis, activity-based coating (ABC), implementation estimation/costing	James L. Lundy. *Lead, Follow, or Get Out of the Way.* San Marcos, Calif.: Avant Books, 1990. David P. Hanna. *Designing Organizations for High Performance.* Reading, Mass.: Addison-Wesley, 1988. Chapter 3. H. Thomas Johnson. *Relevance Regained.* New York: The Free Press, 1992. Chapters 3, 8. James P. Lewis. *Project Planning, Scheduling & Control: A Hands-On Guide to Bringing Projects in on Time and on Budget.* Chicago: Probus, 1991. Chapter 4.

Step Three—The Crux: Establishing the New Direction

Subjects	Sources
Strategy development, project scheduling, organizational development, business performance measurements	Kenichi Ohmae. *The Mind of the Strategist.* New York: McGraw-Hill, 1982. Chapters 10, 11, 16, 17. Peter F. Drucker. *Managing for Results.* New York: Harper & Row, 1964, 1986. Chapters 13, 14. B. Charles Ames and James D. Hlavacek. *Managerial Marketing: The Ultimate Advantage.* Mountainside, N.J.: Managerial Marketing, Inc., 1984. Chapters 15, 16, 17. James P. Lewis. *Project Planning, Scheduling & Control: A Hands-On GUide to Bringing Projects in on Time and on Budget.* Chicago: Probus, 1991. Chapters 5, 7. H. Thomas Johnson. *Relevance Regained.* New York: The Free Press, 1992. Chapter 7. David P. Hanna. *Designing Organizations for High Performance.* Reading, Mass.: Addison-Wesley, 1988. Chapters 4, 5, 6.

Step Four—The Culmination: Working Together for Customers and Profits

Subjects	Sources
Leadership, project management, participative management, teamwork	James L. Lundy. *Lead, Follow, or Get Out of the Way.* San Marcos, Calif: Avant Books, 1990. James P. Lewis. *Project Planning, Scheduling & Control: A Hands-On Guide to Bringing Projects in on Time and on Budget* (Chicago: Probus, 1991). Chapters 9, 12, 13, 14. David P. Hanna. *Designing Organizations for High Performance.* Reading, Mass.: Addison-Wesley, 1988. Chapter 7.

Index

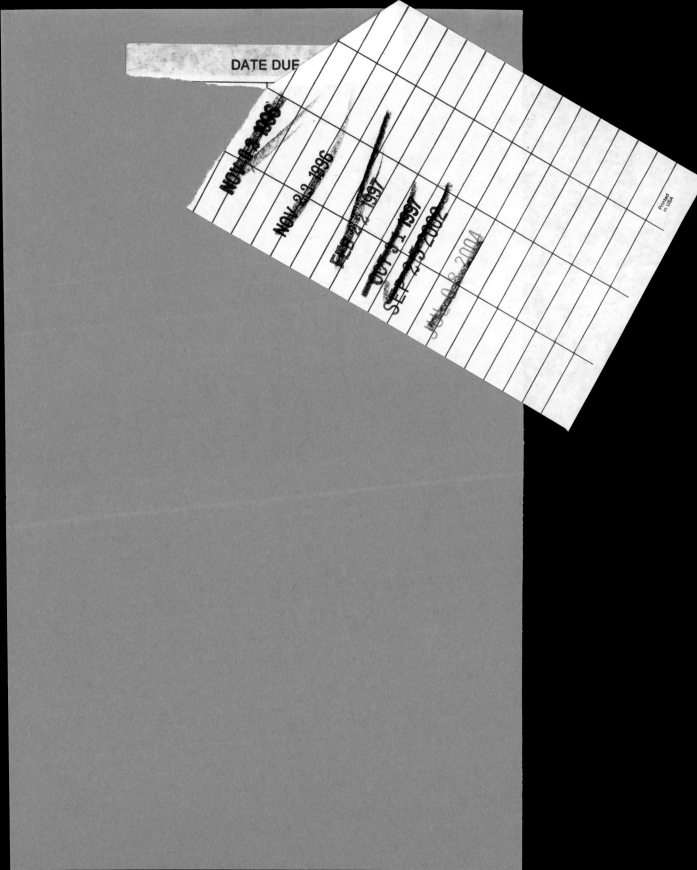

DATE DUE